BIBLE AND GOSPEL

by the same author

A. M. HUNTER

Bible and Gospel

SCM PRESS LTD

334 01613 4

First published 1969
by SCM Press Ltd
*56 Bloomsbury Street London WC*1

© *SCM Press Ltd* 1969

Printed in Great Britain by
Richard Clay (The Chaucer Press) Ltd.
Bungay, Suffolk

| | | 110157 |
| | | Unit Number |

5535-14
Binders Order Number

No. of Vols.	Color 2461	Match Rub ☐	DO NOT WRITE IN THIS COLUMN

| | | Book |
| LETTERING FOR SPINE | | Periodical |

Bible and
Gospel

| | Inches |

| | Extra Lettering |

Hunter

| | Class No. |

| | Oversize |

| | Hand-sewing |

| | Guards |

| | Stubs |

232
H916

| | Head & Tail Lines |

| ☐ Bind as Published | INDEX | ☐ Do Not Trim |
| ☐ Bind as Arranged | ☐ Front ☐ Back | ☐ First Binding |

| | Labels |

COVERS	ADVERTISEMENTS	☐ Match Sample
☐ All ☐ Discard	☐ All ☐ Discard	
☐ One Set ☐ At Back	☐ One Set ☐ At Back	☐ Make Rub
☐ Front Only ☐ In Place	☐ Pure Ads ☐ In Place	☐ Rebind

| | Imprint |
| | Extra Time |

Other Instructions:

Hoff   175531

| | TOTAL |

CHIVERS-TALAN CO.

CONTENTS

PREFACE

This little book, like ancient Gaul, has three parts. Part I is a brief Introduction to the Bible as a whole. Part II deals with the Gospels and the Person and Work of Jesus as recorded in them. Part III deals with what has been called 'the New Quest of the Historical Jesus' as it is presently being pursued in Germany.

Many of these chapters were first given as 'lecturettes' at evening services in Aberdeen churches and inevitably bear the mark of the spoken word. Some of the themes – e.g. the Parables and the Sermon on the Mount – I have already treated at greater length in my published writings; but I have tried always to work over the material anew and improve it. The RSV translation of the Bible is generally used; but where it seems clearer, I have employed the NEB. Occasionally I have done my own translating.

Once again I am grateful to my colleague in the New Testament Department at Aberdeen, Dr I. Howard Marshall, for reading the typescript and correcting some of my errors.

A. M. Hunter

PART ONE

Introducing the Bible

1

The Old Testament

I

Why read the Bible?

It is often said, quite truly, that the Bible is the world's best-seller, but who in fact reads it? Ministers of course, Sunday-school teachers, day-school teachers who give 'Religious Instruction', university students who take 'Biblical Studies' and those devout souls who do their daily Bible readings – isn't that about the lot? For – let's face it – the Book that almost everybody once knew has become the book that practically nobody knows.

Why should this be so?

One main reason is the multiplicity of our modern interests – we simply haven't the leisure our fathers seem to have had for Bible reading. But there are other reasons. The widespread assumption that the Bible, being pre-scientific, is completely out-of-date, is one of them. What light can a book out of the ancient East possibly cast on our problems today, or the way we should live in this turbulent twentieth century whose emblems seem to be the TV screen, the internal-combustion engine and the space-ship? Another reason is that a great many people find the Bible a very hard book to read. For them the prophecies of Isaiah or the arguments of St Paul are so much holy 'double Dutch'. They haven't a clue what the sacred writers are driving at.

And yet I am sure that very many people still cherish a deep, vague reverence for the Bible and that, if they could be shown good reasons for doing it, they might still be persuaded to have another look at what it has to say.

Why then should we read the Bible?

From time to time you hear people talking expansively about the Bible as literature, and suggesting that it is on a par with

Shakespeare. Of course, they are dead right. The Bible as it comes to us in the glorious (if somewhat archaic) English of the 47 men who made the Authorized Version in 1611, is beyond doubt our noblest book of English prose. Read the lament of David for Saul and Jonathan (II Sam. 1) or the fortieth chapter of Isaiah, or that perfect short story about the father and his two sons in Luke 15 (so superbly translated in the New English Bible) or St Paul's 'Song of Songs' in praise of Love, and tell me where you will find majesty, or pathos, or beauty to excel them. And yet, though this is one reason why we cannot afford to be ignorant of the Bible, it is emphatically not *the* reason why we Christians account it the most important book in the world.

What then? You sometimes hear the Bible named 'the Good Book'. A book about goodness? Is it as a sort of text-book on the good life that we ought to study it? Well, every serious-minded person is interested in the problem of right living – wants to know how best he may live out his three score years and ten on the surface of this troubled planet. Is it then because we have in the Bible the supreme text-book on morals that we ought to study it?

Once again, the answer must be No, though now, as the children say, 'we are getting hotter'.

To be sure, there is moral light and leading in the Bible – God's plenty of it. The Ten Commandments, for instance. They are getting pretty old by now; but who will suggest that they are obsolete or irrelevant in a world where crime is on the increase, murder is uncomfortably common and sexual laxity is widespread? Then the Bible contains the Sermon on the Mount, by universal consent the noblest utterance on the moral life in existence. If it is moral light and leading that we are after, where shall we find its equal? And yet this is still not *the* reason why many of us think, with Sir Walter Scott, that 'there is but one Book'.

What then do we find in the Bible that we find in no other book? The answer is, 'The Word from the Beyond for our human predicament'. Let me explain.

When, in the hour of disaster or bereavement, men turn for help to the Bible, do you think that what they are seeking is simply fine literature or ethical light and leading? These things they can find in Shakespeare or the writings of many another clever and wise man of this world. No, perplexed by the burden and mystery of this strange and lovely world, beset behind and before by grief and guilt, and knowing on what a brief and uncertain lease you and I hold the trust of life, they want something that goes further and deeper than this. They want 'a Word from the Beyond for their human predicament'. They want an assurance that, in all their sin and suffering, the Almighty Being who made the world and all things in it really and veritably cares about it all – nay more, that he has *done* something about it, something great and sufficient, something worthy of a God.

And it is just 'this Word from the Beyond for our human predicament' that the Bible, and no other book, claims to give. For the Bible declares not only that there is a God, but that he so cares for us that, once in history, he came right down among us as a man to show us what he is like, and then died on a Cross that we might have forgiveness for our sins and eternal life.

Here is how the great Aberdeen scholar, William Robertson Smith, put it when he was on trial for heresy: 'If I am asked why I receive scripture as the Word of God, I answer with all the Fathers of the Reformed Church: Because the Bible is the only record of the redeeming love of God, because in the Bible alone I find God drawing near to man in Christ Jesus and declaring to us, in him, his will for our salvation, and this record I know to be true by the witness of his Spirit in my heart, whereby I am assured that none other than God himself is able to speak such words to my soul.'

II

The Bible as the Word of God

A true and noble answer, yes; but it raises two connected questions which we must settle before we go further. The first one is: In what sense is the Bible the Word of God ?

Well, the Bible nowhere calls itself 'the Word of God'. The Bible says that 'the Word of God came' to the prophets in the great hours of Israel's history, and that it 'was made flesh' – became human – in Jesus Christ. It would be wiser to say that the Bible conveys the Word of God, or, more simply, that God speaks to us through the Bible. This delivers us from the view, still held by some people, that every word in the Bible, having been written down to some kind of Divine dictation, is completely free from error. No thoughtful Christian can believe this. If it were true, it would make God responsible for every little mistake in scripture as for example in Mark 2 where 'Abiathar' is wrongly written for 'Ahimelech'. If it were true, it would put the book of Leviticus on the same level of inspiration as the Gospel of John.

Yet, if we reject this view, we are just as sure as those who hold it that God speaks to us through the Bible, or, to put it otherwise, that the Bible is the record of a unique revelation to men. Let me take an illustration. Everybody knows what the letters HMV stand for. If you buy an HMV record, you are told that you can hear master Caruso, the greatest tenor of all time. Will you really hear Caruso's voice? Of course, and yet you will also hear some other things – noises made by the machine and by the needle scratching on the disk, which are not 'the Master's Voice'. So it is with the Bible. It makes the real Master's Voice – God's voice – audible to men. But there are incidental noises also – jarring sounds and little flaws – simply because God speaks to us through frail and fallible men – men like Moses or Isaiah in the Old Testament and Peter or Paul in the New. But only a fool will listen to these incidental noises, or be put off by them, when he can hear the Master's Voice.

The importance of the Bible is that God speaks to us in this way through its pages. This is why we say it is the record of revelation, the record through which God makes himself known to us. We believe that when we take the Bible seriously, God, through his Spirit, speaks to us from its pages and that, if we have learnt from the Bible the idioms of God's speech, God can speak to us today in our own lives and in contemporary events.

III

The Old Testament as Christian scripture

Our second question is this: Since we are Christians, not Jews, why should we not stick to the New Testament, and leave the Old Testament to the Jews?

This is not a new question. It is as old as the second-century heretic Marcion who wanted to 'scrap' the Old Testament. It is as modern as Hitler and the Nazis who wished to do the same thing. And many intelligent people, neither heretics nor Nazis, ask the question, Why the Old Testament?

Why then do we reckon it as Christian scripture and bind it up in our Bible with the New Testament Gospels and Epistles?

First, because the Old Testament was Christ's Bible. In it he found revealed the long purpose and deep scope of God's salvation – God's invasion of his race by words and deeds of gracious power.

Second, because 'the Old Testament is the lexicon of the New'; the indispensable dictionary to it. All the great New Testament words – 'Gospel', 'Covenant', 'Christ' and so on – go back to the Old Testament and cannot be understood without it. So too New Testament doctrines like those of 'the Kingdom of God' and redemption through suffering have their roots in the Old Testament. To throw away the Old Testament would be to throw away the key to the New.

But there is more to it than this.

Jesus himself said that he came not to destroy the Law and the Prophets, but to fulfil them (Matt. 5.17). His ministry was to be the crown and completion of the old revelation of God. And the Old Testament is Christian scripture both as history and as prophecy.

It is Christian scripture as history, because, after declaring God's creation 'in the beginning' (Gen. 1.1), it goes on to tell the story of God's people and his dealings with them through the centuries, until in the fulness of time the Saviour came. It is Christian scripture as prophecy because, through the prophets, the Old Testament, 'in many and various ways' (Heb. 1.1), promises and prefigures the salvation realized in Christ and his Church. For we must never forget that it is the same God who speaks to us in both Testaments, and that the God of Abraham, Isaac, and Jacob is the Father of Christ.

5

All this means that the Bible, for all its sixty-six books, is a unity[1] – one great story in two instalments – in which the Old Testament is related to the New as Promise to Fulfilment. 'These are they', said Jesus of the Old Testament scriptures, 'that bear witness to me' (John 5.39).

IV

The story of the Bible

The best way to grasp the truth of this is to go quickly through the story the Bible tells – the story of God's People and his gracious purpose for them.

To begin with, however, remember that for the men of the Bible God is the Lord of history – the God who is known by what he does in the affairs of men. What we call 'revelation' comes through history, and it is the business of the men we call prophets to supply a kind of spiritual commentary to the march of events, and to show men what God is doing and saying in them. Let me illustrate what I mean. Sometimes when a friend of ours does something fine and perhaps unexpected, we say, 'So-and-so's action was a revelation to me'. His act gives us an insight into his nature, shows us what he is really like. Just so the Hebrews held that events in history disclosed what God was like – were a revelation of his character and will.

Now take a further step. It is true that God is present at all times and in every place. But the Bible teaches that God visits the earth decisively in the great crises of history. (The Greek word *krisis* means 'judgment'.) Now in the history which the Bible records there are three great crises which stand out as types of all lesser ones. They are: the Exodus, about 1300 BC; the Exile, 586 BC; and the coming of the Kingdom of God, AD 30.

We are going to study these crises, but let us start further back, as the Bible itself does. The Bible begins with a Prologue, Gen. 1-11, which describes the Creation and the Fall and sets the stage for the story to be unfolded in the rest of its pages. (We shall discuss the Prologue later.) The story of God's saving purpose for

[1] See note at the end of this chapter on the unity of the Bible.

men begins in Gen. 12.1: 'Now the Lord said to Abram, Get thee out of thy country.' God tells Abraham of his purpose to use him to bless 'all the families of the earth'. (Here we get a first hint that God means Israel to be a source of blessing to the whole world.) In obedience to God's call Abraham leaves the security of Ur of the Chaldees (modern Mesopotamia), and goes out not knowing whither he goes. (Here we see the essence of faith: it is a kind of venturing upon vision.) The Bible goes on to tell how eventually his descendants found their way, under Joseph, into Egypt. There Pharaoh turned them into slaves and made their bondage bitter. The first crisis is beginning, its prophet and key-figure Moses.

There follows the familiar story of the Exodus and the crossing of the Red Sea. When their fortunes were at the lowest ebb, God raised up Moses to lead the Israelites out of Egypt, and at the Red Sea wrought a great deliverance for them. 'The Lord caused the sea to go back by a strong east wind' (Ex. 14.21). Even if we explain what happened as a natural, though very unusual, happening, the Bible is clear it was the Lord's doing – a miracle. Tide, wind and panic all contributed to what the Israelites said was the act of God. During the Second World War we talked about 'the miracle of Dunkirk'. Just so the Israelites talked about the miracle of the Red Sea. The Lord had rescued his people with a mighty hand, and this signal deliverance, passing into their song and story, became a type, or symbol, of the yet greater deliverance God would one day work for his people.

From the Red Sea the Israelites marched under Moses to Mount Sinai in Arabia. There God made a covenant (or agreement) with them. 'I will be your God', said the Lord, through Moses, 'and you will be my people' (Ex. 24). The Ten Commandments represent Israel's part of the bargain: they set forth what God requires of his people.

Thus the little people of God, conscious that God had chosen them for his service, and that they in turn had certain obligations to fulfil, had taken the first decisive step on the way to the promised land of Canaan.

What followed is told in Numbers, Deuteronomy and Joshua. Israel, rebelling against Moses' leadership, fell into idolatry and was doomed to wander in the Wilderness for forty years. When Moses died before reaching Canaan, Joshua succeeded him; the Jordan was crossed; and at Jericho the first Canaanite fortress went down before them.

Let us move on now to the books of Judges, Samuel and Kings. After the conquest of Canaan came the time of the Judges (i.e. leaders of the various tribes in war and peace): Gideon and Barak, Samson and Jephthah: then of the Kings, first Saul, then David, then Solomon. On Solomon's death (*c.* 930 BC) the kingdom was divided for and against the house of David. In the north Israel began a new dynasty; in the south Judah kept David's sons on the throne. In the northern kingdom of Israel, however, under King Ahab and his Sidonian queen Jezebel, the people began to forsake the true God and to serve Baal – to worship the gods of the soil. It was then that the prophet Elijah and, after him, Elisha, arose to recall Israel to her true allegiance. After them Amos, Hosea and Micah – the first of the *writing* prophets – warned Israel that their sins must bring down on them God's judgment. The judgment fell in 721 BC when Samaria, Israel's capital, fell and the Assyrians carried Israel into captivity. Thus the northern kingdom perished and its people became known to history as 'the ten lost tribes'.

There remained the southern kingdom of Judah. For the next hundred years, while Assyria threatened it also, prophets, of whom Isaiah of Jerusalem[2] was the greatest, tried to recall king and people to the worship of the true God and to holy living. A partial reformation did indeed come under the good King Josiah in 621 BC (see II Kings 22, 23) when the book of Deuteronomy,[3] setting forth the principles of God's covenant with his people, was found in the Temple. Then, a few years later, Assyria herself was overthrown by Babylon whose menacing shadow fell ever more darkly over Judah as the years went by. It was then that Jeremiah, who saw the second crisis coming, pleaded in God's name with king and people to submit to Babylon. They refused to listen. The crisis culminated in 586 BC when Nebuchadnezzar of Babylon took Judah captive and destroyed Jerusalem and its Temple (II Kings 24, 25).

Had God's purpose for his people completely failed? No, said

---

[2] Isa. 1-39.   [3] Or at least a portion of it.

Ezekiel and the second Isaiah (Isaiah of Babylon), God still has a future for them and the exiles will return. It seemed a thing incredible which nevertheless befell. Fifty years later Cyrus of Persia, who had defeated their old enemy Babylon, issued an edict permitting the exiles to return (Ezra 1). One psalmist put it thus:

> When the Lord turned again the captivity of Zion,
> We were like men that dream,
> Then was our mouth filled with laughter
> And our tongue with singing.
> Then said they among the heathen,
> 'The Lord hath done great things for them'. Ps. 126.1f.

The five following centuries, which bring us down to the time of Christ, we might call the period of the 'Zionists'. The story, so far as the Bible tells us, is told in the books of Ezra and Nehemiah: how the returning exiles, prompted by the prophets Haggai and Zechariah, rebuilt first the Temple and then, years later, the city walls; and how, resolved to be a holy nation living according to God's law, they purified their worship, and, in a passion for racial purity also, prohibited all mixed marriages with foreigners. (It was in protest against this policy of *apartheid* that the books of Ruth and Jonah were written. The first tells how Ruth, a foreign woman from hated Moab, became a noble wife and mother in Israel and the ancestress of the great King David. The other tells how when a Jewish prophet, Jonah, labelled his God 'made in Israel', the Almighty showed him that he cared for Gentiles no less than Jews.)

But, alas, in their zeal to be God's holy people the Jews forgot that through them God planned to 'bless all the families of the earth', and their narrow nationalism brought its own nemesis when one foreign conqueror after another put Israel under his heel. After the Persians came the Greeks under Alexander the Great and his successors; and after the Greeks the Romans under Pompey; and, with the exception of a short spell of 'home rule' under the heroic Maccabees, Israel remained a vassal to foreign powers.

So far as the Old Testament is concerned, the story of the people of God seems over, and the end seems to be disaster and not deliverance. Ah, but this is to forget the magnificent 'forward look' of the prophets. Though Israel may seem 'down and out', they are quite sure that God has a purpose for his people which will eclipse all the glories of their past, and that, as God is God, he will surely accomplish it. Deliverance will come when he finally brings his Kingdom (Isa. 52) and his Messiah (Isa. 9, 11, Zech. 9); there will be a new and greater Exodus (Isa. 35, 40); a new and better covenant (Jer. 31); God will yet pour out his Spirit upon all flesh (Joel 2; Ezek. 36); and all nations will share in his salvation (Isa. 45, 66).

That time – the time of salvation, the time of the Kingdom and the Messiah, of the New Covenant and the outpouring of God's Spirit – did come. It came with the coming of Jesus the Messiah. This will be the theme of our next chapter. In it we shall see how Jesus fulfilled the ancient prophecies and, in living them out, 'crucified' them.[4] But the crucified reality, we believe, is better than all the images of prophecy.

In this sense the Old Testament is fulfilled in the New. But there is another way of talking about 'fulfilment', less theological perhaps, but nevertheless pure Gospel. Christ, we may say, is the Answer not only to the predictions of the prophets but to all the unfulfilled longings of every sinful or sad soul in old Israel. Think of all those who like the psalmist cried, 'Wash me thoroughly from my iniquity and cleanse me from my sin'. Think of all those who like Job cried, 'O that I knew where I might find God'. Think of those disillusioned souls who like the writer of Ecclesiastes cried 'Vanity of vanities! All is vanity'. Think of every earnest soul who like Saul of Tarsus tried by keeping of the Law of Moses to find peace with God – and failed.

All these were crying out for a Divine Answer. And that Answer is Christ. For Christ is 'God's Word from the Beyond for our human predicament' – God's Word, or saving Purpose, made flesh. And to all those today who like those in old Israel cry out for

---

[4] The Fulfiller was other and greater than the prophesied one. Jesus was not the Messiah that many in Israel had hoped for. The Kingdom he brought was established not by the fiat of Omnipotence but by an ignominious death on a Cross. And the salvation he brought was rejected by his own people, so that the vineyard was taken from Israel and given to others.

cleansing from their sins, or a solution to the world's riddle, or a pledge that death does not sever, it is the message of the Gospel that Jesus Christ is God's Yes – the Divine Answer to their prayers.

> The kingdoms of the world go by
> In purple and in gold,
> They rise, they flourish and they die
> And all their tale is told.
> One kingdom only is divine,
> One banner triumphs still,
> Its King a Servant, and its sign
> A gibbet on a hill.

NOTE ON THE UNITY OF THE BIBLE

Without the Old Testament the New Testament does not begin to make sense.

(i) Every page of the New Testament has words or phrases – Messiah, Son of Man, New Covenant, 'Christ our Passover', etc. – which send us back to the Old Testament for clues to their meaning.

(ii) Next, from Genesis to Revelation we can trace a series of biblical patterns or recurring themes which bind the two Testaments together. To say this is not to revert to a *mechanical* view of the Bible's unity which tries to find Christ everywhere in the Old Testament or, like St Matthew, tries to track down literal fulfilments of the Old Testament in the New Testament, e.g. Isa. 7.14 fulfilled in the Virgin Birth (Matt. 1.25). Rather is it to hold an *organic* view of the Bible's unity – to see it as the story of one long unfolding purpose of God from Genesis to Revelation.

Consider, for example, three of the threads that run through the great tapestry of the Bible:

(*a*) the idea of the *covenant* (or relationship between God and man, in which God takes the initiative). We find this first in the story of Noah, in Abraham (Gen. 15), in the old covenant made at Sinai (Ex. 24), in Jeremiah's prophecy of a new covenant (Jer. 31), and in Christ's words at the Last Supper.

(*b*) the idea of the *Exodus*, i.e. of God as Saviour of his people, can be traced from the story told in Exodus, through II Isaiah's promise of the new Exodus, to the 'exodus', or deliverance, of the Cross and Resurrection (Luke 9.51), to St Paul's comparison of Christ and Baptism (I Cor. 5.7, 10.2) to the Passover and the Christian transition from death to life, which is a kind of crossing of the Red Sea.

(*c*) the idea of *'the Day of the Lord'*. We find it first in Amos, then, in apocalyptic form, in Joel and Daniel, then in 'the day of the Son of Man' in the Gospels, and finally in Paul's concept of 'the day of Christ'.

All these subsidiary themes converge on a greater one running through both Testaments – God's gracious coming to man in mercy and judgment. So the Old Testament becomes the indispensable record of the preparation for the Incarnation, for God becoming man in Jesus Christ.

(iii) This brings us to our third and final point. If we are to understand the titles Jesus applied to himself, or the apostolic writers applied to him, we cannot do without the Old Testament. Thus we cannot understand Jesus' favourite title for himself 'the Son of Man' or his mission as God's suffering Servant unless we go back to Dan. 7 and Isa. 53. Nor can we understand his claim to be 'the light of the world' (John 8.12. Cf. Matt. 5.14) without Isa. 42.6 and 49.6.

Again, John 1.1. needs Gen. 1.1 to explain it. 'For St John the Word which had expressed God's will and purpose in creation and in Israel's story has now come to earth in Jesus.' If Paul calls Christ 'the wisdom of God' we need to go back to Prov. 8 and perhaps Job 28. If the Writer to the Hebrews depicts Christ as the Christians' 'great high priest', we can only understand what he means against the background of Jewish sacrificial practice. If the early Christians express their *Credo* in the formula 'Jesus is Lord', we need to remember how the LXX used the word *Kyrios* to translate the name of God.

Thus the New Testament writers think of themselves as the inheritors of the promises made to Israel as the people of God. (Paul calls the Church 'the Israel of God'.) For them Abraham was no obscure and ancient patriarch but the founder of the divine commonwealth to which they belonged. The Gospel, or *kerygma*, of the apostles was that 'the scriptures had been fulfilled', that the hopes and prayer of the Old Testament saints had now come true. The mission and vocation of Old Israel had passed to the new Israel, the Church of Christ, now called to fulfil the world mission that God had set before the old one.

If all this is so, church history may be said to begin not with the apostles but with Abraham. The Ten Commandments are a true part of our Christian heritage. And the Psalms are not merely a Jewish hymn book but 'new songs of praise' for men who worship the God of the patriarchs who is also the God and Father of Christ.[5]

[5] On this whole theme see Dr William Neil's essay in *The New Testament in Historical and Contemporary Perspective*, 237-259.

2

The New Testament

I

The Bible, we said, is the Story of the People of God – a story in two instalments which we call the Old and New Testaments, a story which can best be told in terms of three great crises – the Exodus, the Exile and the Coming of God's Kingdom.

When we had to break off, it was very much an unfinished story: indeed, to all except those with the strongest faith it must have seemed the story of the complete failure of God's purpose for his People.

We come now to the third and greatest of the crises. It is the record of how God fulfilled his promises made through the prophets in a crisis which finalized all previous ones. Of this crisis John the Baptist was the God-appointed herald and forerunner. It is the crisis which began in the reign of the Roman emperor Tiberius when Jesus of Nazareth appeared in Galilee announcing that the time was fulfilled, God was about to set up his eternal Kingdom, and calling on all to repent and accept the good news (Mark 1.15). In short, it is the crisis of the coming of the Kingdom of God and the birth of the new Israel, which is the Church of Christ: a crisis of both blessing and judgment: judgment for old Israel which, by rejecting God's Messiah, forfeited its claim to be the true People of God, and blessing for all, whether Jews or Gentiles, who by accepting Jesus as the promised Saviour, obtain the salvation which he brings.

It is with this climactic crisis in God's dealings with men – and all its repercussions – that the 27 books of the New Testament – Gospels, Acts, Epistles, Apocalypse – are concerned.

We start with the four Gospels, which tell the story of Jesus the Messiah, the Son of God, for the crisis began in what we call the

Ministry of Jesus. Paradoxical as it may sound, what Jesus said and did from the day he was baptized in Jordan to the time when he was crucified on Calvary and raised from the dead, *was* the inauguration of the Reign of God, God acting in his royal power, God visiting and redeeming his People. Jesus is indeed the promised Messiah – the Bearer of God's Rule to men – but such a Messiah as the Jews had never dreamed of, a Messiah who knows he must tread the sombre path marked out for Isaiah's Servant of the Lord, a Messiah who comes 'not to be served but to serve and to give his life as a ransom for many' (Mark 10.45).

We need not rehearse in detail the story which the Gospels tell – the Baptism by John in Jordan, the Temptation in the Wilderness, the Ministry in Galilee, with its preaching, teaching and healing, the confession of Peter at Caesarea Philippi, the transfiguration on a mountain-top, the march on Jerusalem to die . . .

What the story means is that God is offering the blessings of his Kingdom to old Israel, the People whom he chose, through his Messiah. But old Israel will not hear; and Jesus calling twelve men (the number, notice, of the tribes of old Israel) founds the new Israel which is to inherit God's promises and do for the world what old Israel had failed to do. In an Upper Room in Jerusalem, on an April evening in AD 30, by means of broken bread and outpoured wine, Jesus pledges his twelve men a share in the blessings of the New Covenant – God's New Order – soon to be sealed by his death. Then events take their awful course. The Messiah is arrested, tried, condemned, crucified, buried. When darkness falls on the first Good Friday, it looks as if God's great saving purpose for his people proclaimed by Jesus, embodied in Jesus, had been finally defeated. The Messiah in whom all hope of redemption rested lies buried in Joseph of Arimathea's rock tomb . . .

But no, there is a sequel, a most astounding sequel. On the third day after his crucifixion the tomb is found empty; the crucified Messiah appears again to his followers and commands them to preach the salvation he has procured to all men, promising them 'power from on high' to fulfil their task. Seven weeks later, on the day of Pentecost, the promise comes true, the Holy Spirit descends on the waiting disciples and the new People of God, the Church of the risen Lord, goes forth from the Upper Room conquering and to conquer.

The *Acts of the Apostles*, which follows and forms a bridge between the Gospels and the rest of the New Testament, and the 21 epistles, written by Peter, Paul, John, James and the rest, tell how Christ's apostles, or special messengers, led by the risen Lord and filled with the Holy Spirit, carried the Gospel from the Holy City to the Capital of the world; and how, with the founding of little congregations all over the Middle East – in Corinth, Philippi, Ephesus, Thessalonica, etc. – the Catholic, or Universal, Church was set up. Of all the apostolic letters Paul's *Epistle to the Romans* is the greatest. It is the apostle's answer to the question 'What is Christianity?' and is undoubtedly the most important letter ever written. The other letters show how these congregations faced the problems of Christian living in their pagan environments, learning by their mistakes and sufferings, learning too in the course of hard practice the sufficiency of their faith, the radiant adequacy of their hope, the reality of their love.

Thus God's promises to the prophets were fulfilled; God's Reign was inaugurated through his Son, the Messiah; the new Israel came into being with a new Exodus (Luke 9.31) and a new Covenant, and was empowered by God's Holy Spirit for its mission to the world, which is nothing less than the taking of the good news of God's salvation in Christ to all men.

What we call 'church history' now begins. This is the period of God's dealings with men in which you and I are now living. We live 'between the times' – between God's D-Day and his V-Day – between the time when God inaugurated his New Order by the Cross, the Resurrection and the coming of the Spirit, and the Day of the final victory of God when, in ways past all our imagining, God will wind up the scroll of history, make a final end of sin and death, and consummate his purpose revealed in Christ in the glories of another world. Then the full meaning of what God did for us when he sent his Son will be unveiled, we shall see God and his Christ 'face to face', and the faith and patience of his saints will be rewarded.

This is the event of which the last book in the New Testament, the book of *Revelation*, written by John the Seer on the isle of Patmos, tells in its strange but haunting visions:

I saw a new heaven and a new earth (21.1).

They shall not hunger any more, neither thirst any more; the sun shall not strike them, nor any scorching heat. For the Lamb in the midst of the throne shall be their shepherd, and he will guide them to springs of living water; and God shall wipe away every tear from their eyes (7.16f.).

This, then, is the Story of the Bible. We Christians believe that Christ is, as St John says, God's Word, or Saving Purpose, made flesh, become human. Do you remember how wonderfully Browning's Arab physician Karshish puts it to his friend Abib –

'The very God! Think, Abib, dost thou think?
So the All-great were the All-loving too;
So, through the thunder, comes a human voice
Saying, 'O heart I made, a heart beats here!
Face, my hands fashioned, see it in Myself!
Thou hast no power, nor mayst conceive of Mine,
But love I gave thee, with myself to love,
And thou must love Me, who have died for thee.' [1]

We believe that in Christ God has given us his master-clue to the riddle of the world; that God is working out a great and gracious purpose for us and for all men, and that he will surely bring it to a blessed conclusion. Till that day dawns, we are called as members of Christ's Body, which is the Church, to witness to the salvation he has wrought, to summon all men to be reconciled to God through Christ, and by our work and worship, by our service and suffering, to testify whose we are and whom we seek to serve.

II

True or false?

Is the long story we have been telling basically true, or is it just pious fiction?

[1] Robert Browning, *The Epistle of Karshish*.

The first thing to be said in answer is that the Bible never set out to be an ordinary text-book of history. What its writers set out to do was to trace the guiding purpose of God in a series of events that befell a special people. They were writing theological history – history as God gave the prophets to see it.

The next point to remember is that many parts of the Bible which we tend to take literally were never meant to be so taken. The writers of the Bible were Orientals who used poetry, parable and myth in order to convey truth. We will talk presently about the story of the creation and the fall in Genesis. Meantime, for an example, consider the story of Christ's Temptation as told by Matthew and Luke. To take that story with Occidental literalness and think of some physical confrontation between Jesus and a flesh-and-blood devil is to miss the point. This is the story of a searching spiritual experience – a real, not a sham, fight – told by one who was a supreme master of parable.

Does this mean then that there is no real, solid, verifiable history in the Bible, but only poetry, parable, symbol? No, indeed: the Bible is rooted in real history, and at various points we can use the discoveries of the archaeologists to check or confirm people and events mentioned in the Bible.[2]

Here are ten examples from the Old and New Testaments. Excavations begun at Ras Shamra in 1929 have taught us much about the Canaanites who were in Palestine before the Hebrews entered it, and particularly their worship of the fertility god Baal against which the prophets thundered.

The Tell el-Amarna letters, found last century in Egypt, record the invasion of Palestine by the Hebrews.

A century ago an Englishman and his dog discovered in Jerusalem the quarries where King Solomon got the stones to build his temple.

Some letters from a commander to an officer in the Judean town of Lachish go back to Nebuchadnezzar's siege of Jerusalem in 588 BC.

An inscribed cylinder confirms the statement in Ezra 1 that

[2] On this whole subject the best short book is W. F. Albright's *Archaeology of Palestine*.

Cyrus of Persia issued an edict permitting the Jewish exiles in Babylon to return home.

The Dead Sea Scrolls, discovered in 1947 at Qumran, have much to tell us about the Jewish sect of the Essenes who lived and worked near John the Baptist in the Judean Wilderness.

Papyrus documents unearthed from old Egyptian rubbish heaps, if they do not completely corroborate Luke's story of a Roman census at the time of Christ's birth, show at least that one was held about AD 6 when Quirinius was legate of Syria.

In the thirties of this century the long-lost Pool of Bethesda – a double pool in fact, with a rocky gangway in the middle – where Christ healed the man who had been crippled for 38 years, was laid bare for the modern tourist's inspection.

An inscription found in 1961 at Caesarea on the coast of Palestine bears the name of Pontius Pilate. More interesting still, under a convent in Jerusalem men have laid bare the 'Pavement' where Pilate took his seat when he was judging Jesus.

Another inscription found at Delphi, near Corinth, records that the Roman governor Gallio probably arrived in Corinth in the summer of AD 51, and so enables us to say that St Paul reached Corinth, 18 months earlier, in AD 50.

But if the Bible is basically fact, not fiction, we must repeat our first point, which is that the biblical writers were concerned not with tracing the sequence of events but with noting the unfolding of a purpose – God's purpose for his People. This is because they have been taught by the prophets to see history not as a mere catalogue of events and dates but as the scene of the acts of the living God. And what they offer us is the record of certain high points of illumination – certain periods which were supremely significant – the Exodus, the Exile, the Coming of the Kingdom – because in them the meaning of all history is revealed.

The Bible, therefore, is an interpretation of history and an invitation. As interpretation, it tells us of the purpose for which the world exists and of the nature of its Creator and his gracious designs for men. Indeed, it sees history as the battleground of great moral and spiritual issues in which we are constantly being challenged to take sides – for or against God's purposes. And the

Bible is an invitation because, having put forward this interpretation as a reasonable deduction from the facts, it invites us to accept it and make it our own.

III

Right and wrong ways of reading the Bible

We come finally to the practical question: What is the right way to read the Bible? For here, as everywhere else, there are wrong ways as well as right ones. Let us begin with three wrong ways.

First, the 'lucky dip' method. You put in your hand at random and are guided to the text meant to give you light on your particular problem. Though I have heard a distinguished admiral telling the General Assembly of the Church of Scotland how he made such a 'lucky dip' before a great naval battle, I do not recommend it, because it regards the Bible as a collection of magical oracles. If you tried it, you might be like the man who found his text for the day to be 'He went and hanged himself'. The poor chap tried again, and this time his text was 'Go and do thou likewise.'

A second wrong way is to begin at the beginning and plod right through the Bible from Genesis to Revelation. You have probably heard of people who did this – who waded through the Bible as others might wade through the various parts of *The Forsyte Saga*. If you tried this way, you would probably find the Bible a very strange kind of novel, with of course many 'purple passages' in it, but also many dreary deserts in between the oases. Long before you had reached the minor prophets, let alone the epistles of St Paul, you would probably have decided to 'skip' large sections of it through sheer boredom, and to read on a selective principle, which would have been your way of wisdom from the start.

A third wrong way to study the Bible is to regard it as a scientific text-book, which is what it was never meant to be. You maltreat the Bible if you put, say, the first chapters of Genesis alongside Charles Darwin's *Origin of Species* or Fred Hoyle's *Nature of the Universe*. The man who said that the Bible teaches you 'how to go to heaven, not how the heavens go' had the right idea. Science is concerned with *how* the universe works and how life develops.

The Bible is concerned with *why* there is a universe at all and such a thing as human life.

Take the first chapters of Genesis. What is their main point? That the world was made in six days of twenty-four hours each? No, the vital words come first: 'In the beginning God created . . .'. Gen. 1 invites us to contemplate the wonder and mystery of the created world, to believe that God is its Maker, and that he has given man a status in it different from that of other created beings. So too with the story of the Garden of Eden. 'Adam', observe, is the Hebrew word for 'man', and Gen. 3 is to be regarded as a true myth[3] or parable about man. In other words, though Eden is on no map and Adam's fall fits no historical calendar, Gen. 3 describes a dimension of human experience as real now as at the dawn of history. In plain prose, we are fallen creatures, and the story of Adam and Eve is the story of Everyman – of you and me. The Bible goes on to tell in those first eleven chapters of Genesis, which form a (theological) prologue to the whole Bible, how God turned the Man and the Woman out of the garden. A little later (Gen. 6.11f.) we read, 'The earth was filled with violence, for all flesh had corrupted their way on the earth.' And is not this, unhappily, the fact? And if we want further evidence, do we need to look further than the morning paper? Or into our own hearts?

What, then, did the Lord God do about it? The answer fills the rest of the Bible; but two lines from Newman's hymn sum it up:

> A second Adam to the fight,
> And to the rescue came.

What then is the right way to read the Bible? To regard it as 'the only record of the redeeming love of God' and to study it with all the helps modern scholarship puts in our hands.

This means first reading the Bible in a good modern translation like *The Revised Standard Version* or *The New English Bible*. Why is it important to use a modern translation? Because the plain

---

[3] 'Myth' in this sense does not mean fairy tale (like Jack and the Beanstalk). The religious 'myth' corresponds to something which is really true but cannot be expressed in the language of prose or science because it concerns the transcendent or ultimate.

fact is that the Authorized Version, made three and a half centuries ago, is often obscure and difficult for the ordinary reader today. If the Bible is to come home to modern man with living power, it must speak to him in language he can understand.

Having acquired a good modern translation, how do we set about our Bible reading?

The old way was 'a chapter a day'. If you choose this way, I can recommend *The Bible Day by Day* which goes through the whole Bible and prescribes a suitable reading for every day in the year.

The other way is to choose a particular book of the Bible and go systematically through it with a simple modern commentary. There are many of these: *The Layman's Bible Commentaries*, the *Torch Bible Commentaries*, William Barclay's *Daily Bible Readings* and the Scripture Union's *Bible Study Books*.

Where should you start? My answer would be: with the *Gospel of Mark*, which is the earliest of the four. Only when you have a sound knowledge of the story of Jesus does the Old Testament fall into its proper place as a preparation for Christ. From Mark you might go on to *John's Gospel* which is in a sense the key to the first three and the profoundest of them all. After that you might turn to the *Acts of the Apostles*, and read how the apostles carried the Good News from Jerusalem to Rome. Having made this New Testament start, you might go back to one of the historical books of the Old Testament – say, *I and II Samuel*. or *I and II Kings*. Then study one of the prophets – *Amos* or *Jeremiah*. Before you return to the New Testament you might read some of the great Psalms (e.g. 8, 19, 23, 42, 46, 51, 90, 107, 121, 139) so full of the language of true religion. Having done this, you might then come back to the New Testament and study one of Paul's letters. Here *Philippians*, 'the epistle radiant with joy', is the best one to begin with. But when you get to know and love the apostle, have a shot at mastering his magnum opus, *Romans*. Thus, with every book of the Bible you will find your knowledge growing, and you will discover your faith resting on ever surer foundations.

A word in closing. One of the saddest things about the world today is the number of men and women who drift from youth to age with no sense of what life is for or where it is going. For them man seems to be not a creature 'made in the image of God' but just 'an eddy of purposeless dust', and what we call history just one darned thing after another'. It was not always so. For our forefathers –

> Life was real, life was earnest
> And the grave was not the goal.

In other words, life had for them meaning and purpose – and everlasting horizons. Where did they get this meaning and these horizons? They got them from the Bible on which they were nurtured from their earliest days. And we are never going to get that sense of purpose and eternal meaning restored to our lives until we get back to the Bible.

PART TWO

Jesus and the Gospels

3

The Four Gospels

The Gospel before the Gospels

Gospel, a fine old English word from 'god spel' – 'good news' –
exactly translates the Greek word *euangelion* ('evangel'). By the
Gospels we mean the four written records of the Good News
which came into the world with the coming of Christ, for we must
never forget that Jesus came not simply to preach the Gospel but
that there might be a Gospel to preach.

Life always precedes literature, and the Good News about
Christ was being preached long before a single scrap of Christian
literature existed. But if the first Christians had no written Gospels
(the only scripture they possessed was the Old Testament) they
had a *kerygma*. This rugged Greek word means a 'proclamation',
a message to proclaim, and we know that the gist of it ran something like this:

God's promises made through the prophets are now being
fulfilled.

The long-expected Messiah, born of David's line, has come.

He is Jesus of Nazareth, who went about doing good and
performing miracles by God's power; was crucified according
to the divine purpose; was raised by God from the dead and
exalted to his right hand.

He will come again in glory for judgment.

Therefore let all repent, be forgiven, and receive the Holy Spirit.

In the beginning then was the *kerygma*; and this message was
the earliest Gospel with which Christ's apostles went out, as they
said in Thessalonica (Acts 17.6), to 'turn the world upside down.'
Inevitably there would be differences of emphasis in this early
preaching, according as it was addressed to Jews or to Gentiles;

27

but on its essentials the apostles were agreed. 'Whether then it be I or they (Peter, James, John and the rest)' Paul told the Corinthians, 'it is in these terms we preach and in these terms you believed' (I Cor. 15.11).

Of course this proclamation I have outlined must have been filled in by the earliest preachers; and if we ask with what, the answer is: with stories about Jesus' works and words. There was no lack of these, for many 'were still alive'[1] who had heard or seen Jesus in the days of his earthly ministry, and could repeat stories of what he had done and said: how he had healed the sick, befriended sinners, stilled the storm, blessed little children, fed a great multitude, and so on. Indeed, in every big centre of early Christianity there must have been circulating stories about Jesus which the Christians passed on to each other at their meetings for worship or their common meals, and which the apostles used when they preached the Good News to the unconverted.

But what of the teaching of Jesus? Our outline of the *kerygma* said nothing about this. Yet it would be wrong to suppose that the early Christians forgot or ignored the sayings and parables of him who 'spoke as never man spoke'. On the contrary, the sayings of Jesus were treasured for the guidance they gave on the problems of Christian living. (This is how Paul is found using them in his letters – see I Cor. 7.10, 9.14, etc.) Thus from the beginning men remembered the wonderful words of Jesus, prizing them no doubt for their own sake – because they were *his*, the words of their living Lord – but also for their practical value. And about AD 50 somebody – it *may* have been the apostle Matthew – put together a collection of Jesus' sayings to serve as a pattern of Christian behaviour for all who had accepted Christ as Saviour and Lord. (Our scholars call it 'Q' – from the German word *Quelle*, 'source'. Matthew and Luke used it when composing their Gospels. Though the actual document has not survived, we can roughly reconstruct it.[2])

Thus the materials later to be incorporated in our written Gospels took shape in the generation that followed the Crucifixion and Resurrection. This was the period of the *oral* tradition – the

[1] About AD 55, when Paul wrote I Cor., most of 'the five hundred brethren' who had seen the risen Christ 'were still alive' (I Cor. 15.6).

[2] See my book, *The Work and Words of Jesus*, 131-146.

time when men still preferred 'the living and abiding voice' of eye-witnesses to any written record.

But this time could not go on for ever. When a generation had gone by – a generation when the apostles carried the Gospel from Jerusalem to Rome – the situation began to change. Many of the eye-witnesses had now 'fallen asleep'; some, like James the Lord's brother, had been martyred. Now it became increasingly important that the truth about Jesus should be set down in writing before the time should come when there would be none left to say, 'I remember Jesus in the days of his flesh.' Besides, converts were flocking into the young churches who needed instruction in the Christian faith. In short, the need for a written record of the work and words of Jesus began to be felt; and with the need came the man.

II

The Four Gospels

The man who, as the poet put it,

> first found grace to pen
> The life which was the Life of men

was John Mark, a native of Jerusalem, a close friend of Peter and later a companion of Paul. What materials lay to his hand when he took up his pen? To begin with, he possessed a rough outline of the Lord's Ministry in the *kerygma* – an outline that could be filled in with stories about Jesus. Mark probably had his own memories of Jesus during at least his last days in Jerusalem (Mark 14.51 may well refer to him, and be his own modest signature in the corner of his Gospel). He had also received many stories from his friend Peter; and of course many others were current in the Christian circles in which he moved. (We know from Acts 12.12 that the apostles used his mother's house as a place of rendezvous.) With these, in Rome, about AD 65 Mark made his Gospel.

'Vivid' and 'realistic' are the adjectives which best describe the earliest Gospel: 'vivid', because it abounds with what look like eye-witness touches; 'realistic', because Mark depicts Jesus in all his true humanity; and when he comes, after telling the story of the Galilean Ministry, to relate Jesus' Passion in Jerusalem, though there is no morbid dwelling on details, he spares us nothing of its stark horror. But, if we stopped there, we should have told only half the truth. Through Mark's whole record there runs a mysterious undercurrent. There is a mystery about this Man and the Kingdom of God he proclaims. He acts with a unique and superhuman authority. 'Heaven and earth shall pass away,' he says, 'but my words shall never pass away.' He says that he has come to 'give his life as a ransom for many'. Asked by the High Priest at his trial, 'Are you the Messiah?' he answers, 'I am', adding mysterious words about the Son of Man being destined for the right hand of God. When, therefore, we read that the grave could not hold him, we feel that this is the only fitting *dénouement* to the drama. For this is not one more story of the death of a martyr, however good and great. It is, as Mark tells it, the story of Jesus the Son of God, bringing the Kingdom of God through suffering and death and victory over death.

Mark's Gospel soon went into wide circulation. To the Church's leaders, however, charged with the instruction of new converts in Christian living, it had one drawback: it recorded little of our Lord's teaching. What was needed to remedy this defect was a revised and enlarged edition of Mark's Gospel. Matthew's Gospel, which appeared in Antioch about twenty years later, did just this. Besides adding narratives about Jesus' Birth and Passion, and quoting texts to show that Jesus fulfilled the Messianic hope of the Old Testament, Matthew inserted in his Gospel five great discourses of Jesus, the most important being the Sermon on the Mount. Admirably arranged for its purpose, Matthew's Gospel was to become the most popular of all.

Matthew, a Jewish Christian, wrote for his fellow countrymen. But, about the same time, another man was thinking of the needs of the great world beyond the bounds of Jewry. Had not his friend Paul done more than any other to take the Good News to the Gentiles? Was there not need for another Gospel which would depict Jesus not simply as the Messiah of the Jews but as the Saviour of all men? It was Luke, Paul's friend and physician, who met this need. Himself a Gentile and, to judge by his books, a cultivated and compassionate man, he conceived the plan of writing a two-volumed work on the beginnings of Christianity which would appeal to 'his excellency Theophilus'[3] and other like-minded Gentiles. Volume I, Luke's Gospel, which recounts 'all that Jesus began to do and to teach', has its sequel in Volume II, the Acts of the Apostles, which tells how Christ's 'Special Messengers' carried the Good News from Jerusalem to Rome.

In the course of his travels 'the beloved physician', as Paul calls him (Col. 4.14), had greatly added to his own knowledge of Jesus' works and words, as he had fresh information about his Birth and his Passion. With this new material, the collection of our Lord's sayings which Matthew also used, and some help from Mark's Gospel, he made his book. One thing he wished to do was to set the Story of Jesus against the background of world history – hence the five-fold dating in Luke 3.1ff. One portrait before all he wished to paint for his readers – the portrait of Jesus as the Friend and Saviour of all men, especially the last, the least and the lost. To these aims he brought the gift of a fine Greek style, and the result was what has been called 'the most beautiful book in the world'.

'Last of all, perceiving that the external facts had been made plain in the (other) Gospels, John, urged by his friends and inspired by the Spirit, composed a spiritual Gospel.' So Clement of Alexandria, a famous early church father, wrote about the Fourth Gospel, that according to St John. To set the Story of Jesus forth in its true *spiritual* depth, to see it clearly against the background of eternity, this was John's aim.

Good tradition[4] declares that the Gospel was written in Ephesus, perhaps about AD 80. The early Church ascribed it to the apostle John who probably figures in it as 'the beloved disciple'. Whether the Apostle himself did the actual writing or, as is more probable, left it to one of his disciples, it is neither unscientific nor un-

---

[3] Named in the prefaces to both of Luke's volumes – see Luke 1.3 and Acts 1.1. He must have been a notability of some kind.

[4] That of Irenaeus who had heard Polycarp tell of his intercourse with 'John the disciple of the Lord'.

reasonable to hold that John is the 'authority' behind the Fourth Gospel[5] and that it preserves his recollections of Jesus. At any rate, recent study shows that John's Gospel rests back on ancient, independent and valuable tradition about Jesus which supplements, and sometimes corrects, what the other evangelists have to tell.

What St John sought to do was to win men to saving belief in Jesus as the Christ the Son of God (John 20.31) by bringing out the ultimate meaning of his work and person. After long years of pondering the whole story, he had asked himself, What is the difference Christ's coming means to men? The answer which he sets on Jesus' lips, is 'I came that they may have life and have it abundantly' (John 10.10). Real life, spiritual life, life lived in communion with God, life with the tang of eternity about it, life eternal in this world and the next – a life made possible by the ministry, death and resurrection of Jesus and now mediated through the Holy Spirit – this is the theme of John's Gospel. For Jesus was, as St John puts it in his famous Prologue (John 1.1-18), the Word, or saving Purpose, of God, made flesh.

III

The Trustworthiness of the Gospels

We come finally to the question: Are the Gospels reliable sources of history?

The fact that the earliest of them, Mark, was not written till about AD 65, i.e. a generation after the events, troubles some people. But is it really a serious difficulty? The gap is hardly more than that which separates us from the beginning of the Second World War. Those of us who were in our twenties, or even thirties, in 1939 must still have vivid memories, as I have, of those fateful years. Just so when Mark wrote the earliest Gospel, many were still alive who had been in their prime in AD 30, could remember well what led up to the Crucifixion and the Resurrection, and could check the truth of what Mark had to tell.

[5] In the Bible, if a man has disciples who carry on his work, even after his death, their work may be ascribed to him as 'author'. A good example is the book of Isaiah. See my *According to John*, 106.

But someone will say, 'For a whole generation the Gospel tradition was handed down by word of mouth. Human memories are fallible, and everybody knows that a good story can be "improved" in the telling. Was not the record of what Jesus said and did exposed to the risk of serious distortion in those thirty odd years? How can we be sure that the Gospels are substantially reliable?'

Let me begin my reply by saying that it would be foolish to claim that everything in the four Gospels is equally reliable as history. There are, for example, some narratives peculiar to Matthew – I am thinking chiefly of Pilate's wife's dream, the earthquake, the rising of the dead saints, the descent of the angel at the Resurrection – where, it seems to me, that we are dealing, at best, with Jerusalem gossip or, at worst, with pious embellishment bordering on the apocryphal. But, this said, let me add that, after long years of study, it is the considered verdict of serious scholarship that Mark is a document of high historical value, that Luke is not far behind it as a source, and that John, the most theological of the Gospels, can be shown to rest back on ancient, independent and reliable tradition about Jesus.

There are four sound reasons for believing that our Gospels are substantially reliable.

First: *The earliest Christians carefully preserved the tradition of Jesus' words and works.* Dwell a moment on that word 'tradition'. Today we depend on written or printed records, and the word 'tradition' suggests to us something unfixed, floating and unreliable. It was not so among the Jews or early Christians. For the Jews, fixed and guarded tradition was *the* means for preserving the words of their great teachers, and there was nothing unreliable about it. Their memories were much better than ours because we rely on print, and they were trained to remember accurately as we are not. Now the early Christians, who were Jews, took the same care in preserving what their Lord had said and done. Thus our very earliest sources, Paul's letters (e.g. I Thess. 4.1; I Cor. 15.3) attest the first Christians' concern to transmit faithfully the tradition of their Lord's words and works. Their task was made easier by the fact that Jesus himself had cast much of his teaching, e.g. in the Sermon on the Mount, in poetic form and made his disciples learn it by heart. Moreover, roughly one third of his words took the form of parables, those wonderful short stories that have a way of sticking in the memory.

This is not to claim that everything in the Gospels belongs to fixed and guarded tradition; but it is to claim that in its essentials the tradition goes back to Jesus himself, and that it was handed on by trustworthy persons.

Second: *Our Evangelists were in a position to know the facts about Jesus.*

John Mark, the friend of Peter and Paul, moved, as we might say, in the best apostolic circles where, if anywhere, the truth about Jesus was to be known. Dr Luke tells us in his Preface to his Gospel (Luke 1.1-4) that before he wrote it, he took pains to go right back to the beginning for his facts, consulting those who had been eye-witnesses. St Matthew may have been the man who made the collection of Jesus' sayings which was used in the composition of the first and third Gospels.[6] Eye-witness testimony undoubtedly lies behind the Fourth Gospel which carries the authority of John, the beloved disciple.

Incidentally, one way of convincing yourself that the four evangelists are not mere pious romancers is to compare our Gospels with what are known as 'the apocryphal Gospels' – those highly-coloured accounts of Jesus which began to appear in the second century. Written to satisfy popular curiosity about the childhood of Christ, his Passion and his Resurrection, they abound in obvious fantasy and legend. (Among other things they tell us how the boy Jesus 'Made small fowl out of clay, and blessed them till they flew away', how at his Baptism fire was kindled in Jordan, and how, when he came out of the tomb, the Cross was seen following him.) It is the very absence of these prodigies from our Gospels which is the best evidence of their authenticity.

---

[6] Papias, who wrote very early in the second century, said: 'Matthew compiled the *Logia* in the Hebrew (Aramaic) language and everyone translated them as he was able.' *Logia* means 'oracular utterances'. Reputable scholars like T. W. Manson argue that Papias is referring to the Dominical utterances gathered together in 'Q'.

Third: *Our evangelists give the impression of being honest reporters.*

Mark, it has been said, 'does not spare the Twelve'. On the contrary, he refers again and again to their obtuseness and unbelief. Indeed, he is not afraid to record even Jesus as asking 'Why do you call me good?' (Mark 10.18) – a question which might very easily be misunderstood – or, on the Cross, as crying 'My God, my God, why hast thou forsaken me?' (Mark 15.34). In fact, the story all our Gospels tell is the very reverse of a success story. Nor is any attempt made to iron out discrepancies in the tradition, as anyone quickly realizes who tries to construct a harmony of the Gospels.

Fourth and finally: *through all the Gospels shines one fundamental picture of Jesus, whose authenticity forces itself on every unprejudiced reader.*

Here we may cite two witnesses, neither of whom can be accused of *parti pris.*

The English philosopher John Stuart Mill declared: 'It is of no use to say that Christ as exhibited in the Gospels is not historical, and that we do not know how much of what is admirable has been super-added by the tradition of his followers. Who among his disciples or their proselytes was capable of inventing the sayings ascribed to Jesus, or of imagining the life and character revealed in the Gospels?'

Alongside this testimony set that of Günther Bornkamm[7] the German Form Critic: 'The Gospels', he writes, 'bring before us the historical figure of Jesus in the immediacy of his power. What they report about the message, deeds and history of Jesus is marked still today by an authenticity, a freshness and an individuality – uneffaced by the Church's Easter faith – which carry us back directly to the earthly figure of Jesus.'

What, then, are the features in this picture of Jesus which shine so clearly through the Gospels and their sources? His deep humility before God, and, conjoined with it, his claim to divinely-given authority, and his exercise of it: his complete dedication to the purposes of his Father, and, in the same breath, his complete

[7] *Jesus of Nazareth,* 24.

35

dedication to the service of man: his unerring judgments on the secrets of men's hearts – and his limitless and unconditioned forgiveness of the guilty: his passionate concern for all the needy, the poor and the sinful – all that led in fact to the nickname 'Friend of publicans and sinners' – his unshakable conviction that for them the hour of God's salvation had struck, that he himself was God's chosen instrument in it and that men's fate depended on their relation to himself.

It is features like these which make Jesus everywhere recognizable in the Gospels. The basic historicity of this whole picture impresses itself on the candid reader. Moreover, in order to receive this impression, it is not necessary to be an expert in Biblical Criticism. The impression is pre-scientific. It can be felt by the layman no less than by the professional.

We conclude then that the tradition about Jesus in the Gospels is to be relied on – that it was carefully preserved by the first Christians, that the evangelists were in a position to know the facts, that they reported them as honestly as they could, and that their resultant picture of Jesus has about it an unmistakable impression of authenticity.

Let us sum up our whole discussion of the Gospels. Through all four runs the conviction that Jesus was a quite unique person who did things that passed men's understanding, that his whole ministry was full of the presence and power of God, and that it did not end with his death.

Scientific study of the Gospels does not lead to the conclusion that the original story of Jesus recounted the life and death of an ordinary man, and that later this story was given 'a supernatural twist' by theologians like Paul and John. The writers of our Gospels believed they were witnesses to the life of the Son of God on earth, to his death for men's sins on the Cross, and to his victory over 'the last enemy' death. On this assumption the evangelists tell their story, and on this assumption it makes sense.

Are they right in their assumption? Historical criticism can help us to understand the story of Jesus better. (Its function, as P. T. Forsyth[8] put it, is 'to disengage the kernel from the husk, to save

---

[8] *Positive Preaching and the Modern Mind*, 192.

the time so often lost in the defence of outposts, and to discard obsolete weapons and superfluous baggage'. So it can clear the ground for the erection of a house of doctrine in which the component materials can be chosen according to their real strength.) But, of itself, it cannot answer the question. What the Gospels do is to leave us face to face with the question, 'What think ye of Christ? Whose son is he?' (Matt. 22.42). At this point it is 'Over to us.' How we answer that question is a matter of personal decision for each one of us.

NOTE ON FORM CRITICISM

The early 'twenties' of this century saw the rise in Germany of a new sort of Gospel criticism – *Formgeschichte*, which was englished as 'Form Criticism'; its pioneers being K. L. Schmidt, Martin Dibelius and Rudolf Bultmann. What were their motives, aims and procedures?

A literary criticism which merely seeks to uncover documentary sources behind the Gospels (Mark, 'Q', etc.) is, they argued, not enough. Let us try to reach back behind the documents to *the oral tradition* about Jesus which later found written expression in our Gospels, seeking to discover what 'forms' it took, and why this or that story about Jesus, this or that saying of his, came to be preserved.

It was their contention that in the earliest years the memories of what Jesus had said and done circulated orally for the most part in independent units, or *pericopes*. These memories however were not prized in and for themselves – the early Christians had no biographical interests – they were valued for the help and guidance they gave on the problems and needs of the young churches as they met for worship, engaged in missionary preaching, instructed converts, argued with the Jews and so on. Now, said the Form Critics, invoking the 'laws of tradition' in folk literature, these traditions about Jesus must, through constant repetition, have assumed more or less fixed 'forms', or patterns; and if we study those now preserved in the Gospels we may hope to classify them according to their 'form': sayings and parables, of course, 'pronouncement stories' (like the one about 'tribute to Caesar'), miracle stories (like the tale about the healing of the Leper), stories about Jesus (like the Baptism and the Transfiguration).

The task before the Form Critic is therefore threefold: first, to classify the materials in the Gospels; second, by the removal of additions or changes, to restore them to their original form; and, third, to discover their 'life-situation' (German: *Sitz im Leben*), i.e. the actual concrete occasion for which the young churches formed and used the tradition. If we can do all this successfully, said the Form Critics, we ought to be one stage nearer the historical Jesus.

Alas, in the hands of its earliest practitioners, especially Bultmann, it seemed to work out in the opposite way. As a result of their labours, Jesus seemed to become not nearer but more remote. For if the Form Critics were right, our Gospels were so shot through with the beliefs of the early Christian communities that we could know very little for certain about the historical Jesus.

In this country, largely owing to the historical scepticism of Bultmann, Form Criticism had a very cool reception, only R. H. Lightfoot of Oxford being ready to follow it wholeheartedly. None did more to call Bultmann's bluff (if the phrase may be forgiven) than T. W. Manson. 'It is not Higher Criticism', he said 'but the Higher Credulity that boggles at a verse in Mark and swallows without a qualm pages of pure conjecture about the primitive Christians' psychology and its workings on the pre-literary tradition.'[9] Not all our scholars were equally hostile in their reactions. C. H. Dodd, for example, as his books show, was prepared to admit a positive value in the Form-critical method and to turn it to constructive ends. But, speaking generally, British scholars have had grave reservations about the assumptions, techniques and conclusions of the German Form Critics.

The main counts in their indictment were as follows:

The Form Critics ignored or set aside the accepted results of earlier scholarship.

[9] *The Expository Times*, May 1942, 249.

They wrote as if all the eye-witnesses of Jesus had gone into hiding after the Resurrection.

They assumed that the oral tradition was quite floating, unfixed and unreliable, leaving no place for carefully preserved and fixed tradition.

They drew dubious parallels between oral tradition in other cultures, where the time of transmission is a matter of centuries, and the oral tradition in the early Church, where it is a matter of decades.

They took for granted that the early Church could not distinguish its own teaching from the teaching of Jesus, when we know for a fact that a man like Paul was careful to do so.

They sometimes wrongly assumed that the form of a Gospel story was a sure criterion of its authenticity – or, oftener, its inauthenticity – which of course it is not.

Finally, the Form Critics 'failed to notice that many of the questions which, on the evidence of the Epistles, were hotly disputed in the apostolic age, are not dealt with in the recorded teaching of Jesus, so that the Church cannot be accused of reading its own concerns back into the Gospel tradition.'[10]

Form Criticism is now nearly fifty years old. How stands it now in the eyes of the scholars?

Turn first to Germany, the land of its origin. Here Form Critics still flourish; but, we are told, because the results of Form Criticism were so inconclusive, 'the mention of literary "forms" as such has largely passed out of scholarly discussion of Gospel passages, even in Germany'.[11] On the other hand, the pupils of Bultmann are steadily retreating from the extreme views of their master. Whereas Bultmann could once affirm that the Gospels yield us little historical information about Jesus, his former student Bornkamm[12] tells us that 'they are brimful of history'.

We turn next to Sweden. There, some dozen years ago, their leading New Testament scholar, H. Riesenfeld, rejected the

---

[10] G. B. Caird, *St Luke*, 22.
[11] James M. Robinson, *A New Quest of the Historical Jesus*, 37.
[12] G. Bornkamm, *Jesus of Nazareth*, 26.

Form Critics' theory of Gospel origins and propounded a new one of his own. The Form Critics' contention that our Gospel materials originated chiefly in the evangelistic and instructional needs of the primitive Church is, he said, not proven. This was not the true 'life-situation' of the Gospel tradition. On the contrary, right from the beginning the tradition of Jesus' words and works constituted 'a Holy Word' comparable with the Old Testament, and its transmission was the care of special persons. His argument may be summed up thus: (1) The Jewish community was accustomed to transmit its oral tradition in a relatively fixed and controlled way; (2) New Testament references to tradition show that the first Christians, most of them Jews, had a like concern for the faithful transmission of their Lord's words and deeds; (3) this process of faithful transmission began with Jesus, himself a teacher who made his disciples repeat and memorize his teaching.

This theory, later supported in detail by his compatriot Gerhardsson, is still *sub judice*. Clearly, even if it does not cover all the facts (it would fit the *words* of Jesus better than his *deeds*), there is much to be said for its main thesis that from the beginning Christians were at pains to ensure that the tradition about Jesus should be carefully preserved and passed on.

No comparable new theory of Gospel origins has emerged in this country. The British attitude to radical Form Criticism can be seen in a recent book entitled *Vindications* by a group of Anglican scholars. Its core is a sustained attack on the historical scepticism of Bultmann, with its high-light a devastating critique of a heavily Form-critical commentary on Mark by Dennis Nineham, a pupil of R. H. Lightfoot. (Nineham has since made a spirited reply.) On the other hand, many British scholars have made free and constructive use of Form Criticism, regarding it as a new and serviceable tool in their critical equipment. Perhaps the finest example of this is C. F. D. Moule's *The Birth of the New Testament* in which, while avoiding the excesses of the Germans, he puts the method of Form Criticism to illuminating use.

4

The Kingdom and the Messiah
1 · The Paradox

Let us begin, as Luke does (Luke 3.1), by setting the Ministry of
Jesus against its background in world history. It begins with a
baptism administered by John in the river Jordan, mid-way
through the reign of the Roman emperor Tiberius. Among the
recipients of that baptism was a man called Jesus, from Nazareth.
Born in Bethlehem of Judea in the reign of the Emperor Augustus,
he had grown up in Nazareth of Galilee, learning the trade of a
carpenter. When Augustus died in AD 14, he must have been
about twenty. Doubtless the news of the death of the great
Emperor troubled many of his contemporaries, fearful lest it might
mean the end of the Augustan peace and an orderly empire. But
Jesus was thinking of another peace and another empire. When,
about a dozen years later, the voice of prophecy, so long silent,
rang out again through John the Baptist in the Judean desert,
Jesus knew that his time was at hand. He went down from
Nazareth to be baptized by John in Jordan, and to begin a Ministry
in which he would proclaim a dominion mightier and other than
the Roman. This is the historical setting.

A 'paradox' is something which sounds absurd but is, or may be,
really true. And paradox lies at the heart of the Gospels. It is the
paradox of the Kingdom of God and the Ministry of Jesus. Yet
on our resolving of this paradox depends our understanding of the
story of Jesus.

If we ask what is the central theme of the first three Gospels,
there can be but one right answer: the Kingdom (or Reign) of
God. With this theme Jesus began his Ministry; it is the meaning
of his miracles; it is the burden of his parables; in the thought of
the Kingdom he lives, and works, and dies.

Consider the earliest Gospel. St Mark, after telling us about John the Baptist, relates how Jesus came into Galilee announcing, 'The Kingdom of God is upon you' (Mark 1.15 NEB). And yet, as we read on, the story which unfolds itself is not one of spectacular signs and wonders but of a man preaching, teaching and healing in Galilee, until he has won such a reputation that, after a great open-air meal with his followers, they are fain to carry him off and make him a king (John 6.15, which makes explicit what is implied in Mark's narrative). He refuses and retires to the north-west frontiers of Palestine. When we next hear of him, near Caesarea Philippi, there is secret talk between himself and his twelve disciples about Messiahship, the Son of Man and death; and, six days later, a mysterious incident on a mountain top. Then, as if having taken an irrevocable decision, he moves south with his disciples to Judea and Jerusalem. There, about Passover time, after his cleansing of the Temple, he is arrested by his enemies, tried, condemned and crucified. A few days later his friends are announcing that he has risen from the dead . . .

(Nineteen hundred years after, we may add, this crucified Carpenter, who never wrote a book or left the soil of Palestine, has nine hundred and fifty million followers.)

This briefly is Mark's rather puzzling story. How can it be the story of the coming of the Kingdom of God? The very phrase suggests the power and glory of God being manifested in such a royal way that all may know that he is God. Yet all we see apparently is a Galilean Carpenter turned itinerant prophet who draws after him a motley mob of publicans, prostitutes and sinners and ends his life on a gibbet, the sport of passers-by, while his twelve closest followers forsake him and flee. Can the career of this Carpenter conceivably be the inauguration of the Kingdom of God? This is the paradox.

Obviously our first summary will not do. There are things in this story – hints and happenings pregnant with meaning – which we have missed – or glossed over – and, missing, have failed to understand the story. Let us try again, beginning with Jesus' Baptism.

I

The story of what befell Jesus at Jordan must have come to the disciples from Jesus himself; for, according to Mark, nobody else saw or heard the really important happenings there. First, a heavenly voice said to Jesus, 'Thou art my only son, in thee I am well pleased.' The words come from Ps. 2.7 and Isa. 42.1. One is the coronation formula of the Messianic King of Israel; the other the ordination formula of the Isaianic Servant of the Lord. This remarkable combination cannot be fortuitous. It was his own destiny Jesus saw in the Messianic King of Israel and the lowly Servant of the Lord. At his baptism Jesus was made aware that he was called by God to be the Servant Messiah. He was born to suffer, born a king.

The other extraordinary feature of the Baptism was Jesus' vision of God's Spirit descending on him. Again we are reminded of Isaiah's Servant of the Lord: 'I have put my Spirit upon him' (Isa. 42.1). In the Bible, Spirit means creative, divine power. The descent of the Spirit means that from this time Jesus knew himself to be equipped with divine power. Here we may find the secret of the astonishing authority which informed his later words and works.

If we were to put the meaning of the whole event in one sentence, would it not be: 'The ordination of the Servant Messiah'?

II

Now consider the words with which Jesus opened his Ministry. 'The time has come; the Kingdom of God is upon you; repent and believe the Gospel' (Mark 1.15 NEB). It is a proclamation that men are living in a quite unique hour of history, that God is initiating a new era in the record of his dealings with them.

'The time' (*ho kairos*) means 'the appointed time'. What time determined in the counsels of God is this? Go back again to Isaiah, chapters 40 and 52, and you will find the answer. There the prophet foretells the 'good news' (*b'sorah: euangelion*) – the gospel – of the coming of God's Reign:

> Look, 'tis the feet of a herald
> Hastening over the hills
> With glad, good news,
> With tidings and relief,
> Calling aloud to Zion,
> 'Your God has become King!' (Isa. 52.7. Moffatt)

No doubt Isaiah expected this day of God's Reign to dawn soon. However, in the providence of God, the stream of this great hope was to run underground for five centuries till 'the appointed time' came. It came in the reign of the Roman Emperor Tiberius when Jesus appeared in Galilee, saying in effect, 'The time which Isaiah prophesied is now here.'

If the first incident said, 'This is the ordination of the Servant Messiah', the second says, 'God has begun to reign.'

III

Consider, next, the Galilean Ministry itself. We have tended to think of it as a time of quiet teaching and preaching in contrast with Jesus' later career in Judea when he is marching on the Cross – the time of his Passion which we might equally well call his Action. Yet we misunderstand this earlier time if we picture it simply as a peaceful pastoral wherein the serene wisdom of the Teacher accorded well with the flowers and birds of Galilee. Something of Whittier's 'sabbath rest by Galilee' there may have been about the Ministry, but surely more of Bunyan's 'Holy War'. We ought to picture the Galilean Ministry not statically but dynamically. Jesus did not say that he was come to teach but to cast fire – holy fire – on the earth. It is not a colloquium but a campaign on which he is engaged.

His words bear this out. He begins his Ministry by announcing that he is sent to 'proclaim release to the captives'. He compares his mission to the binding of the strong man – the devil – by a stronger one. To his returning missionaries he cries, 'I saw Satan fall like lightning from heaven' (Luke 10.18). And all through his Ministry there rings a note of terrible urgency as though a crisis uniquely fraught with blessing or with judgment for 'this generation' were upon them.

Only if we see the Galilean Ministry thus do we see it aright; and the emergent picture of the chief figure in the campaign is not that of some Galilean Sage or Socrates teaching truths of timeless wisdom, but of 'the strong Son of God', armed with his Father's power, spear-heading the attack on the devil and all his works, and calling men to decide on whose side of the battle they will be. 'The Kingdom of God is in your midst' (Luke 17.21). 'The Kingdom of God exercises its force' (Matt. 11.12)[1]. 'If I by the finger of God cast out demons, then is the Kingdom of God come upon you' (Luke 11.20).

Our third study, therefore, shows us the Kingdom of God at war with the kingdom of evil, with Jesus heading the assault. Looking back at the Ministry years after, St John saw it thus: 'The Son of God appeared for the very purpose of undoing the devil's work' (I John 3.8 NEB).

IV

Pass now to Caesarea Philippi (Mark 8.27-33). The Galilean Ministry has climaxed in the Feeding of the Five Thousand, at which, clearly, popular excitement was running high and many were fain to take Jesus by force and make him a King Messiah after their own worldly dreams. Thereafter, probably in flight from the dangerous enthusiasm of his friends, Jesus has retired to the north-west borders. But the battle joined in Galilee must be finished in Jerusalem (Luke 13.32f). So, before he moves south, Jesus makes sure that his disciples understand the issues. In the solitude of Caesarea Philippi, almost in the shadow of snow-capped Mount Hermon, he asks them: 'Who are men saying that I am?' They reply that popular speculation takes various forms. 'But you,' he says, 'who do *you* say that I am?' At once Peter utters the thought in all their minds. 'You are the Messiah' – the Deliverer long promised by God through prophet and seer. The right answer? Yes, and Jesus tacitly accepts it, but he goes on: 'The Son of man must suffer and die before he comes to his triumph.'

Observe, he says 'the Son of man', not 'the Messiah'. This is

[1] For this translation see T. W. Manson, *The Sayings of Jesus*, 134.

not, as was once supposed, merely another way of saying 'man' (as in Ps. 8.4). On the contrary, as a piece of self-description there could hardly be a higher one. For 'the Son of man', a phrase ultimately derived from Dan. 7.13, is a mysterious Man[2] who receives a kingdom from God and is destined to reign as God reigns. With this majestic figure Jesus identifies himself; yet, in the same breath, insists that suffering and death await him, because God wills it so. To Peter, with his hope set on some sort of worldly Messiah, the very idea is repugnant. He rebukes Jesus, only to be himself in turn rebuked with awful severity. Peter is conceiving Messiahship in man's terms, not God's. What Jesus means is this: 'Peter, you find the very thought of a suffering Messiah abhorrent? Yet this is the way God's Reign works, and God's great vice-regent though I am, I must travel the road marked out for the Suffering Servant of the Lord. There is no other way, and you must be ready to suffer also.'

Six days later follows another incident (Mark 9.2-8) closely linked with Peter's confession, yet so mysterious that to this day we hardly know how to begin explaining it. On a mountain – no doubt Mt. Hermon – as he prays (Luke 9.29), Jesus is transfigured with an unearthly radiance. From the unseen world appear Moses and Elijah talking with him (Luke 9.31) 'about the *exodus*' – the deliverance – which he must accomplish at Jerusalem. And the bewildered disciples hear a heavenly voice reassuring them, 'This is my Son, my Beloved, listen to him' (Mark 9.7 NEB).

Our fourth study therefore says: 'The last battle between the Kingdom of God and the kingdom of evil must be joined: and it will involve the death of God's Messiah.'

V

Pass now to Jerusalem, to the Last Week, to the Last Supper. Jesus has entered the Holy City 'in lowly pomp'. He has cleansed the Temple. He has also predicted its destruction. Now it is Thursday night, and in the quiet of 'a large upper room' Jesus meets with the Twelve for a final meal together (Mark 14.22-25. Cf. I Cor. 11.23ff.).

[2] See special note at the end of this chapter.

To understand what follows, recall certain things. If the occasion is a supper, Jesus had likened the Kingdom of God to a supper (Luke 14.16-24). Moreover, this particular supper is either an anticipated Passover meal, or the Passover itself. Now the Passover commemorated the great act of God which initiated the first Exodus and led to Israel's being marked out as God's special People by a covenant at Sinai sealed with blood. But Jesus, declaring that the Jews were no longer God's people (Mark 12.9), had, by word and deed, spoken of the creation of a *new* Israel. Yet before this could be, the Son of man, as God's Servant, must 'give his life as a ransom for many' (Mark 10.45); and his coming Passion he had compared to a 'cup' to be drunk, a cup in which his disciples might somehow share (Mark 10.38).

Now notice what he does in the Upper Room. First, he takes a loaf and breaks it, handing it to the Twelve with the words: 'This is my body (which is for you).' Then he delivers the cup to them, with the red wine gleaming in it: 'This cup is the (new) covenant in my blood.' And he invites them to eat and drink.

By setting apart the bread and wine, Jesus is offering his disciples a pledge of the Kingdom of God soon to come 'with power' (Mark 9.1) through his sacrifice. In describing the broken bread and the outpoured wine as his body and blood, he is not only claiming to embody that Kingdom but is representing, in vivid symbol, that sacrifice of his own life 'for many' which he is soon to accomplish in fact. By inviting his disciples to eat and drink of the bread and wine, so interpreted, he is giving them a share in the power of the broken Messiah.

The 'new covenant' (Jer. 31.31ff.) which must be ratified by the Servant's death (Isa. 42.6, 49.8, 53) has been symbolically inaugurated and in a few hours' time will be sealed in blood and in fact. Then the work of the Servant Messiah, begun at his water-baptism in Jordan, will be consummated in his blood-baptism (Luke 12.49f.) at Golgotha, that baptism in whose virtue many will share.

Thus the fifth episode is a great acted sign – an effective sign – by which Jesus says: 'I pledge you a share in the Kingdom of God soon to come with power by the Servant Messiah's death.'

VI

Take one last look at Jesus in Mark's Gospel. Betrayed and arrested, he stands before the High Priest on trial. 'Are you the Messiah?' asks Caiaphas. 'I am,' Jesus replies, 'and you will see the Son of Man seated at the right hand of God and coming with the clouds of heaven' (Mark 14.61f. NEB).

It is Jesus' last unconquerable confession of faith in his mission, and he clothes it in words taken from Dan. 7.13ff. (with one phrase borrowed from Ps. 110.1), 'There came with the clouds of heaven', Daniel had written, 'one like a son of man, and he came to the ancient of days, and was presented before him. And to him was given dominion and glory and a kingdom.' This is the key of Jesus' reply to Caiaphas. Despite the apparent ruin of his cause Jesus predicts its triumph. What he predicts is vindication and enthronement. He will be received to the highest place heaven affords, and this his exaltation and triumph they shall know.

In our last study Jesus therefore says: 'The Servant Messiah's victory is assured.'

Was the Servant Messiah vindicated? Did 'the purpose of the Lord prosper in his hand'? Did he 'prolong his days'?

The Christian answer is not doubtful. It affirms that Jesus conquered death, and that by his resurrection he 'opened the kingdom of heaven to all believers'.

Later we shall discuss the Resurrection. Meantime, let us see how the story of Jesus looks after these six studies from Mark. We have tried to fill in the bare outline of Mark from which we began, dwelling on 'the hints and happenings pregnant with meaning', and interpreting them with a depth exegesis.

As a result we are driven to two very important conclusions.

1. *You cannot tell the story of Jesus without a theology*. The old liberal scholars, depicting Jesus in purely human terms, tried to tell his story without dogma. (How little they had to say, for example, about the reasons for Jesus' death on the Cross!) It was Schweitzer who, for all his aberrations, taught us that we cannot tell Jesus' story without talking christologically. (If we try, we shall end up with one more martyr, however good and great –

with a Jesus not nearly big enough to explain Christianity.) Without the theology (and this includes christology and eschatology) the story does not make sense. And the key to most of the theology is in the Old Testament, especially in the Psalms, the Servant Songs of Isaiah and the book of Daniel.

2. The second conclusion is not less important. Let us lead up to it by recapitulating two points:

(*a*) Jesus believed the Kingdom of God to be present in himself and in his ministry – present in a 'mystery', see Mark 4.11, 'To you the secret of the Kingdom of God has been given' (NEB) – but none the less really present and active.

(*b*) No less clearly he saw his Ministry, from Jordan to Golgotha, as a fulfilling of Isaiah's prophecies of the Servant of the Lord.

Put (*a*) and (*b*) together and you get a terrific paradox, a paradox which, we know, gravely perplexed Peter and the other disciples, and indeed only became luminous with meaning after the Resurrection. Time and time again Jesus sought to initiate them into its truth, supremely on the road to Jerusalem – witness Mark 10.42-45. What he was trying to let them into was the Messianic Secret – the Secret not of who Messiah was – they had already divined this – but of what he must do and suffer.

But the secret, the mystery, the paradox – what is it? Quite simply, the Ministry of Jesus as the Servant Messiah, from Jordan to Calvary, *is* the Kingdom of God, God acting in his royal power, God visiting and redeeming his people. For the Kingdom of God is no earthly empire to be set up by a political *coup d'état*. It is a Kingdom in which God rules redeemingly through the Ministry of Jesus: not something added to the Ministry but the Ministry itself. The suffering and the sacrifice of Jesus the Servant Son of Man, so far from being only a prelude to the triumph, are the triumph itself, a triumph which the Resurrection will clarify and reveal.

St John saw this when he depicted the Cross as the 'glory' of Jesus; but the first heralds of the Gospel were not blind to it when they said in their preaching that in the ministry, death and resurrection of Jesus the Kingdom of God had been inaugurated.

We have been talking, some will think rather academically, about the *Mysterium Christi* in the Gospels. But, as my old teacher A. J. Gossip used to say[3], and rightly, Jesus is not primarily an academic problem to be solved, but a life lived out, a dream of God come true, God's Amen to men.

NOTE ON THE SON OF MAN

Much has been written about the title Son of man. Let us set down briefly what we believe to be the truth about it.

For a clue to its meaning we naturally turn to the Old Testament and Jewish literature, where we find it bears a variety of meanings. It occurs very often in Ezekiel where it means 'man' – a human being – over against almighty God. Thus, 'Son of man, stand upon your feet', says God to the prophet, 'and I will speak with you' (Ezek. 2.1). On the other hand, in Ps. 80.17 it stands for *Israel*:

> But let thy hand be upon the man of thy right hand,
> The son of man whom thou hast made strong for thyself.

In the famous vision of Dan. 7, after the appearance of four beasts symbolizing successive despotic empires, there comes, 'with the clouds of heaven, one like a son of man', symbolizing 'the saints of the Most High' – the people of God – to whom God gives sovereignty and dominion without end. Finally, in *The Similitudes of Enoch* (an apocalyptic tract of uncertain date) Daniel's representative, or societary, figure of the Son of man seems to become less of a symbol and more of an individual.

When we turn to the Gospels, we find the phrase 'the Son of man' many times on Jesus' lips, and his alone. In most cases it refers to himself. Some instances are of a quite general kind, e.g. 'the Son of man came eating and drinking' (Matt. 11.19); but, for the most part, the Son of man sayings group themselves round two main motifs: (*a*) humiliation, as 'The Son of man must suffer many things' (Mark 8.31); and (*b*) exaltation, as 'You will see the Son of man seated at the right hand of God and coming

[3] H. Anderson, *Jesus and Christian Origins*, ix.

with the clouds of heaven' (Mark 14.62, with a clear echo from Daniel).

How shall we explain Jesus' use of the term?

1. He probably derived the title from Daniel, as he deliberately made it his favourite name for himself. Why? First, it was *mysterious*, even ambiguous. Its Aramaic original *barnash* could serve as a substitute for 'I' – compare Ps. 34.6, 'This poor man cried'. Thus 'no term was more fitted to conceal, yet at the same time to reveal to those who had ears to hear, the Son of man's true identity'[4] – his Messiahship. Second, since it was weighted with a truly human pathos, it enabled Jesus to declare his kinship with the poor, the sinful and the unfriended (Luke 19.10). Third, it signified his special role as the Bearer of God's Rule and the predestined Head of the new Israel he was creating.

2. Jesus interpreted the title *in terms of Isaiah's Servant of the Lord*. 'The Son of man', he said, 'came not to be served but to serve and to give his life as a ransom for many' (Mark 10.45). In other words, Jesus knew himself called of God to fuse in his own person and destiny the two roles of the Son of man (Daniel) and the Servant of the Lord (Isaiah).

3. Even when Jesus used it as a title – and he could so use it without overtly claiming to be the Messiah – its strongly corporate overtones made it not merely a title but an *invitation* to join him in the destiny he had accepted[5] (cf. Luke 9.59).

---

4 M. Black, *An Aramaic Approach to the Gospels and Acts*[3], 329.
5 See G. B. Caird, *St Luke*, 94, 130.

5

The Kingdom and the Messiah
2 · Corollaries

In our last chapter we studied the terrific paradox at the heart of
the Gospel story – that the ministry of Jesus was in fact the
inauguration of the Kingdom of God. Now we must draw out the
corollaries of the paradox; for only so shall we begin to understand
the meaning of the Church, the Christian ethic, the person of
Christ, the Cross and the Christian hope.

But before we come to the corollaries, we must dwell a little
further on the meaning of the Kingdom of God.

Modern men have had their own ways of interpreting the
Kingdom of God, and mostly they have gone astray. Some have
taken it as the biblical equivalent of the doctrine of evolution on
the principle of

> Some call it evolution,
> And others call it God.

Others have interpreted it as some earthly Utopia to be built by
men on the principles of Jesus. And some Roman Catholic scholars
have had a way of equating it with the Church. They are all of
them wrong.

The Kingdom of God (*Basileia tou theou*) means the Rule or
Reign of God; and if we are to understand it, we must think of it
not territorially, or statically, but *dynamically*. It means the living
God acting in his royal power, God regnant and redeeming, God
visiting and redeeming his people. We may define it as the
sovereign activity of God in saving men and the new order of
things thus established.

Now the Kingdom of God, so understood, was for the Jews *the*
great hope of the future. Another name for the Messianic Age, it
connoted the whole salvation of God, the Event in which the
whole long travail of history would find its final meaning and God

would complete his saving purpose for the world.

Jesus, as we saw, opened his ministry by declaring that this Reign of God was now dawning. The *Eschaton*, or End Event, for which the Jews had been praying through the centuries, was now breaking into history. This is what our scholars call 'inaugurated eschatology'; and if we study the works and words of Jesus in the Gospels, we can see what is meant by it.[1]

First, we have sayings which declare that the Kingdom is a present reality. 'If I by the finger of God cast out devils, then is the Reign of God come upon you' (Luke 11.20). 'The law and the prophets were until John: since then the good news of the kingdom of God is preached' (Luke 16.16). 'The Kingdom of God is in your midst' (Luke 17.21). Second, we have sayings of Jesus which declare that the old prophecies of the Day of the Lord are coming true: 'Blessed are the eyes that see what you see. For I tell you, that many prophets and kings desired to see what you see, and did not see it, and to hear what you hear, and did not hear it.' (Luke 10.23f.). Third, Jesus' miracles of healing are, as he told the Baptist, signs of the presence and power of the Kingdom. 'Go and tell John', he said to his messengers, 'what you have seen and heard. The blind are receiving their sight, the lame walking, lepers are being cleansed, the dead are being raised up, and the poor having the good news preached to them' (Luke 7.22). Finally, Jesus' parables one after another – the Sower, the Seed growing secretly, the Leaven, the Seine Net, the Great Supper – all presuppose the Reign of God as a present reality. All of them, observe, compare the Rule of God not to some inert, static thing, but to something in movement, or to somebody doing something; and each of them says, in its different way, to those who have ears to hear, 'God is now amongst you in his royal and redemptive power. Now is the day of salvation.'

To the corollaries and consequences of all this we must now turn.

---

[1] For a fuller discussion of the evidence see my book *The Work and Words of Jesus*, Ch. 10.

I

The first concerns the King in the Kingdom which has been inaugurated. When Middleton Murry[2] said, 'The secret of the Kingdom of God was that there was no King – only a Father', his paradox contained truth. *The King in the Kingdom Jesus proclaimed was a Father.* 'When you pray, say Father . . . thy Kingdom come' (Luke 11.2). 'Have no fear, little flock,' he told the disciples, 'your father has chosen to give you the Kingdom' (Luke 12.32 NEB). 'My Father', he said, 'has appointed a Kingdom for me' (Luke 22.29).

But here a word of warning. So accustomed are we Christians to address God in prayer as 'our heavenly Father' that we are apt to imagine that God's Fatherhood was the new and momentous truth which Jesus came to declare and which he broadcast wherever he went. A study of the Gospels will not bear this out.

When he was addressing God, Jesus used the Aramaic word *Abba* (Mark 14.36). Now you will search Jewish sources in vain for a parallel to this. Jesus' usage is unprecedented. What research shows is that *Abba* ('Dear Father' 'Daddy') was the word Jewish children used in talking to their human fathers; but no God-fearing Jew would have dared to apply this 'caritative' – this term of endearment – to the high and holy God. Jesus was the first to do this; and if there were no other evidence, this alone would testify to his sense of unique sonship.

But, though Jesus called God *Abba*, he did not go about saying to the crowds in Galilee, 'God is your Father and you are all brothers.'[3] For Jesus the Fatherhood of God was not a theological commonplace to be bruited abroad to all and sundry. He spoke of God as Father to a chosen few and in private; and if we ask why, the answer is, because the experience of God as Father was the supreme reality – the last and deepest secret – of his own life, and we cannot speak lightly to all the people of the things that most profoundly move us.[4]

Nor did Jesus, as men have supposed, go about teaching God's

[2] *The Life of Jesus*, 37.

[3] In the earliest Gospel, Mark, Jesus speaks of God as Father only four times, always to the disciples, and always after Peter's confession.

[4] See T. W. Manson, *The Teaching of Jesus*, Ch. 4.

universal Fatherhood – as though we were all, by some inalienable
birthright, sons of God. As he spoke of God as his own Father, so
he taught that men might *become* sons of God. But for this supreme
privilege they must become debtors to himself. Here are his
words: 'No one knows the Father but the Son and those to whom
the Son may choose to reveal him' (Matt. 11.27 NEB). 'No one
comes to the Father except by me' (John 14.6).

We conclude, then, that the King in the Kingdom was a
Father – a *holy* Father (compare the opening of the Lord's
Prayer: 'Father, *hallowed* be thy name'). But the knowledge of
this Father was not a truth to be shouted from the house-tops, or
even revealed in parables, except in hints – as in his peerless story
of the father and his two sons. Only with the coming of the Holy
Spirit did this secret become an *open* secret. Then the chief word
in Jesus' esoteric vocabulary became the precious possession of all
God's adopted sons; as Paul was to put it to the Christians in
Rome: 'The Spirit you have received is not a spirit of slavery
leading you back into a life of fear, but a Spirit that makes us sons,
enabling us to cry Abba! Father!' (Rom. 8.14f. NEB).

II

The second corollary is ecclesiastical – *the Kingdom of God
involves the Church.*

One of our stateliest hymns begins:

> The Church's one foundation
> Is Jesus Christ our Lord.
> She is his new creation,
> By water and the Word.

But is the Church really Christ's 'new creation'? Some clever
modern men would persuade us that Jesus never intended to
create a Church. One of them, the Frenchman Loisy, said, 'Jesus
proclaimed the Kingdom of God, but the Church came.' Loisy
was wrong. What he should have said was, 'Because Jesus proclaimed the Kingdom of God, the Church came.' For, as convex
involves concave, so does the Kingdom involve a new Israel, a
Church.

E

We are agreed that Jesus proclaimed that the Rule of God had begun. But is God an *émigré* Ruler, a Sovereign without a sphere of sovereignty? And what kind of King is he who has no subjects? The very idea of a Rule of God implies a People living under the Divine Rule, a Church.

Now take a second point. Kingdom and Messiah go together; they are correlates, one implying the other. What I mean is that the basic idea of the Messiah is that he is the Bearer of God's Rule to men. Jesus, as we have seen, knew himself to be God's Messiah, and it is clear from the way he thought about his Messiahship that he envisioned a new community.

For Jesus conceived his work as Messiah in terms of two Old Testament figures, the Son of man in Daniel and Isaiah's Servant of the Lord. Study these figures in their Old Testament contexts, and you will find that both of them are *societary* figures, i.e. they imply a community.

But we can go further. Jesus spoke of himself as a 'Shepherd' and his disciples as a 'flock' (Luke 12.32). Shepherds and flocks were of course a familiar part of the Palestinian scene; but we have here more than simply pastoral imagery. In the Old Testament (e.g. Ezek. 34) and in Jewish literature (e.g. The Psalms of Solomon 17) 'Shepherd' is one of Messiah's names, as the Messiah's task is said to be the gathering of God's flock – the forming of a new community for God.

In view of this it is not surprising that some of Jesus' parables – e.g. The Mustard Seed, The Drag Net, The Wheat and the Tares – have clearly in view the creation of a new *community*, a Church.

All this is what might be called the theological theory of the matter. Let us now turn to the Gospels and see Jesus translating the theory into fact, into persons.

First: *Jesus called twelve men and taught them.* Twelve was the number of the tribes of Israel. What Jesus is doing is creating a new Israel, and instructing it – instructing it in what Paul was to call 'the law of Christ' (Gal. 6.2).

Second: *Jesus sent the Twelve out as heralds of the dawning Kingdom.* What was the purpose of their mission? Let us recall that the Rule of God is something dynamic. It creates a people wherever its power is felt. Jesus' purpose, then, in sending out the Twelve, is the ingathering of God's People; and there is evidence enough in the Gospels that it did not fail.

Third: *When Jesus held the Last Supper, it was an act in the establishment of the Church.*[5] Recall his 'eucharistic words' (I Cor. 11.23-25): 'This is my body which is (broken) for you.' 'This cup is the new covenant in my blood.' By means of broken bread and outpoured wine, Jesus gives his disciples a share in the 'new covenant' to be inaugurated by his death. Long before, at Sinai, God had constituted the Hebrews into a People of God by making a covenant with them. The 'new covenant', now prophetically inaugurated in the Upper Room, implies the creation of a new People of God, a new Church. On the night of the Last Supper the Twelve sat round the table as the nucleus of the new Israel, that community which sprang into effective life after the Resurrection and on the day of Pentecost was empowered by God's Spirit for its task. So began the *Ecclesia*, the new People of God, the Church of Christ, now the greatest society on earth. Jesus' prophetic parable of the Mustard Seed has come true: the seed has grown into a great tree.

III

The third corollary is moral – *the Kingdom of God involves a new style of living*.

If Jesus preached the coming of God's Kingdom, he also taught his disciples. What is the connexion between the preaching and the teaching? The ethical teaching of Jesus is his design for life in the Kingdom of God. It is as if he were saying to his men, 'Since the Kingdom of God has dawned and you are in it, you must live in a Kingdom way.' What we call the ethic of Jesus is a pattern of living – direction rather than directions – for all who belong to the Kingdom of the Father.

Of this moral teaching the most compendious summary is the Sermon on the Mount (Matt. 5-7; Luke 6.20-49), which we shall discuss later. Here it will be enough to make two points about it.

[5] K. L. Schmidt, in *T.W.N.T.* III, 521.

First: the ethic of Jesus is not a new code of laws on whose perfect keeping our salvation depends. If it were, we would all be doomed to damnation, since none of us measures up to it. Rather is it an *ethic of grace* – man's appropriating response to the grace of the God who brings his Kingdom.

Consider the precepts of Jesus in the Sermon. Each and every one of them was preceded by something else – Jesus' proclamation of God's inbreaking Rule and the new relationship with God which this made possible. If Jesus says to his disciples, 'You must forgive', it is because they themselves have already received his assurance, 'Your sins are forgiven.' If he bids them live as sons of God, it is because they already know themselves to be children of Abba, Father. If he commands them to 'love their enemies', behind his command lies the grace of that God who 'makes his sun rise on good and bad alike, and sends the rain on the honest and the dishonest'. Always it is a case of 'Freely you have received, freely give.'

Second: the most distinctive element in Jesus' new style of living is *the commandment of love* – the 'royal law' (James 2.8), the law of the Sovereign who is a Father.

Jesus interprets the whole duty of man to his fellow man in terms of the verb 'to love' (Mark 12.28-34; Luke 10.25-28). Love is the master-key to the morals of the Kingdom. By 'love' Jesus does not mean some kind of sentimental emotion, neither does he mean that we must resolve to 'like' certain people. (In this sense, as the famous stanza about Doctor Fell reminds us, we cannot love to order.) For Jesus, love means *caring* – caring practically and persistently for all who meet us on life's road, caring not merely for the worthy and deserving but for all who need our help, even enemies. This is the new 'law' of the Kingdom, because the King in the Kingdom is a Father who himself cares for the ungracious and the ungrateful.

IV

The fourth corollary is Christological – *the Kingdom is centered in Christ.*[6]

[6] Or, to put it in one word, Origen's, *autobasileia:* 'he is the Kingdom'.

'In the Gospel,' said Marcion with true insight, 'the Kingdom of God is Christ himself.' For it is clear from the Gospels that where Jesus is, there is the Rule of God. Thus, the Kingdom is promised only to those who attach themselves to Jesus' person, and to be discipled to him is to be 'in the Kingdom'. Or consider what is implied by a saying of Jesus like, 'If *I* (the 'I' is emphatic in the Greek) by the finger of God cast out devils, then is the Kingdom of God come upon you' (Luke 11.20). Jesus speaks as one who knows himself to be the Reign of God incarnate.

Why then is the connexion between Jesus and the Kingdom of God not made more explicit in the Gospels than it is? The answer lies in what has been called 'the Messianic Secret'. During his Ministry Jesus refused to publicize his Messiahship; and only at the end, in answer to the High Priest's leading question, did he openly avow it (Mark 14.61f.). The title he preferred was 'the Son of man' – a title ultimately drawn from the seventh chapter of Daniel.

The famous vision of Daniel 7 sets forth the drama of world-history as the seer saw it. Across the stage pass four great world-empires symbolized as beasts. (Do we not still talk of 'the British Lion' and 'the Russian Bear'?) One by one they pass away, and then we read:

'There came with the clouds of heaven *one like a son of man*, and he came even to the Ancient of Days (God pictured as an old man) and was presented before him. And to him (the son of man) was given dominion and glory and a *kingdom*, that all peoples, nations and languages should serve him.'

A verse or two later we read: '*But the saints of the Most High* (the people of God) shall receive the kingdom and possess it for ever.'

Daniel's vision therefore provides the answer to our question, How are Jesus and the Kingdom connected? God gives the Kingdom to the Son of Man (Jesus), and 'the saints' – the disciples of Jesus as the nucleus of the new People of God – receive it from him.

But if this is so, it will not do to take the Son of man in the Gospels as just a poetical way of saying 'man'. It is the title of a heavenly being who receives sovereignty from God himself. When, therefore, Jesus styles himself 'the Son of man', it is a veiled way of saying that he is the Bearer of God's Kingdom to men, and in his Ministry we see that Kingdom embodied and in action. Nor is this all. In Dan. 7 the 'one like a son of man' represents 'the saints of the Most High' – he is the Head of the People of God. So it becomes clear why Jesus promises the Kingdom to his followers (Luke 12.32, echoing Daniel). His disciples are these 'saints', the first-fruits of the new People of God he is calling into being.

But it may be said: 'A heavenly being who receives sovereignty from God' – this is hardly the picture of Jesus in the Gospels. If he has any royal power, it is largely hidden. Instead, we are told that if there is to be sovereignty for the Son of Man, it must be by way of suffering and death. Why so? It is because God has ordained that the Son of Man must fulfil the destiny of Isaiah's Servant of the Lord. It is by the *Via Dolorosa* that Jesus the Son of Man must go to his throne. 'When you have lifted up the Son of man,' says Jesus to his critics in John's Gospel, 'then you will know that I am he.' (John 8.28).

The connexion between Christ and the Kingdom is established. Marcion was not wrong: the Kingdom is Christ. But we are not quite done yet.

Think of God's New Order only as a Kingdom, and its Bearer may well call himself the Son of Man. But for Jesus, the King in the Kingdom is a Father. If he who rules in the Divine Kingdom is a Father, only one word – the word 'Son' – will rightly describe him who brings it to men. This is why the Gospels tell us that Jesus claimed to be the only Son of God (Mark 12.6, 13.32) and why, talking to his disciples, he could say:

Everything is entrusted to me by my Father; and no one knows the Son but the Father, and no one knows the Father but the Son and those to whom the Son may choose to reveal him (Matt. 11.27 NEB).

Here are the raw materials of the highest Christology.

V

The fifth corollary is 'crucial' – *the Kingdom of God involves a Cross*.

Jesus began his Ministry by proclaiming 'The Kingdom of God is upon you.' On the last journey to Jerusalem, he said, 'The Son of man did not come to be served but to serve and to give his life as a ransom for many.' Because he is himself both the Herald of the Kingdom and the Son of Man who must die for 'many', Jesus poses in his own person the problem of the Kingdom and the Cross, and how they are connected.

Half a millennium before he was born, scripture – however adventitiously – had connected the Kingdom and the Cross. For in Isa. 52 and 53 the Herald with the 'good news' has not long done announcing 'Your God has become king' when we read that the Lord's Servant must be 'numbered with the transgressors' in his death for the sins of 'many', before he comes to his triumph. It is the career of Jesus in prophecy.

Some have said that Jesus 'died to bring in the Kingdom'; but since Jesus knew the Kingdom to be, in a real sense, already present during his Ministry, we can hardly put it that way. The Cross must fall *within* the Kingdom – must be part of the redeeming Rule of God, its burning focus and centre, the condition not so much of the Kingdom's coming as of its coming 'in power'.

At his Baptism Jesus must at least have reckoned with death as a possible end to his mission. From Peter's Confession onwards he saw it as an ineluctable necessity: 'The Son of Man', he said, 'must undergo great sufferings . . . and be put to death . . . and rise again three days afterwards' (Mark 8.31 NEB). The Greek word for 'must' is *dei*. It is the *dei* of Divine necessity: God wills the Cross for him; if he is to finish the work his Father gives him to do, there is no other way.

No less than five times in Mark's Gospel (Mark 8.31, 9.12, 9.31, 10.33f. and 10.45) Jesus predicts his Passion. Whenever he speaks of it – whether he refers to 'suffering many things' or 'being delivered into the hands of men' or 'being treated with contempt' or 'giving his life as a ransom for many' – he echoes the sombre

61

language of Isaiah about the Suffering Servant of the Lord. It may be that the phrasing of some of these predictions, notably Mark 10.33f., has been made more precise after the event. But even making allowance for this, we are still left with abundant evidence that Jesus knew that as the Son of man he must be delivered up into men's hands, suffer many things and be killed – as the climax of his career as the Lord's Servant.

This, then, is the problem. In some real sense the Kingdom has come during the Ministry of Jesus. Yet Jesus as the Son of man must die for the common salvation. Two sayings in Mark point the way to its solution.

In Mark 4.11 Jesus says that 'the secret of the kingdom of God' has been given to the disciples. This 'secret' can only be 'the hidden dawn of the kingdom of God itself amid a world which to human eyes shows no sign of it'.[7] In Mark 9.1 he declares that at no distant date men will see 'the kingdom of God already come in power'. That same phrase 'in power' Paul uses in Rom. 1.4 of the Resurrection. But between the coming of the Kingdom 'in secrecy' and its coming 'in power' lies the Cross. The inference is hard to resist that the Cross was necessary if the Kingdom was to become an open secret – a manifest reality. Jesus dies that the Kingdom of God may come 'in power'. If further evidence is called for, we may find it in the parable he told, during the last days of his Ministry, about the Grain of Wheat:

'Truly, truly I say unto you, unless a grain of wheat falls into the ground and dies, it remains alone; but if it dies, it bears much fruit' (John 12.24). His death is the indispensable condition of his Ministry bearing a rich harvest.[8]

The *Te Deum* is right. It was when Jesus had 'overcome the sharpness of death' that he 'opened the kingdom of heaven to all believers'.

VI

Our final corollary is consummatory – *The Kingdom of God, though inaugurated, still awaits consummation.*

The Rule of God has been inaugurated 'in power' by Christ's

---

[7] G. Bornkamm, *Jesus of Nazareth*, 71.   [8] See my *According to John*, 83f.

rising from the dead and the coming of the Holy Spirit. But it is yet to come in finalizing fulness. In other words, if God's D-Day is past, we still await his V-Day, when, all evil vanquished, he will be all in all.

How did Jesus speak of the Kingdom in the future? Some of his sayings seem to refer not to any Kingdom to come on earth but to the eternal order of God where his Rule does not come and go, but is eternally present. Of such are his words at the Last Supper 'I will no more drink of the fruit of the vine until I drink it *new* in the Kingdom of God' (Mark 14.25), and his prediction that 'many will come from east and west to feast with Abraham, Isaac and Jacob in the kingdom of heaven' (Matt. 8.11).

Others refer to a coming of the Kingdom or of the Son of man (the two cannot be separated) *in history*. Thus, as we have seen already, Jesus predicted that the Son of man would rise 'after three days' (Mark 8.31), that at no distant time the Kingdom would 'come with power' (Mark 9.1), and that the Son of man would be seen coming 'with the clouds of heaven' (Mark 14.62). These sayings express Jesus' certainty that he was destined to triumph, and with him the cause of God which he embodied. What they assert is swift vindication after apparent defeat. Of this Jesus was sure.

What actually happened, we know: the Easter victory over death, the coming of the Spirit, the rise of the apostolic Church. A new era had begun. This was the coming of Christ in history, and St John, who interprets Christ's future coming in terms of the advent of the Spirit, was not wrong.

But if there was to be a coming in history, there was also to be another final coming. Thus in one passage (Mark 13.24-26) Jesus speaks of the Son of man's coming 'with great power and glory' against the background of the break-down of the universe. In a second (Luke 17.26-30) Jesus says the end of the existing order will be the signal for the 'revelation' of the Son of man. And in a third (Matt. 25.31ff.) he pictures all the nations – dead as well as living – gathered before the Son of Man when he 'comes in his glory'.

We need not take all this tremendous imagery with prosaic

literalness, since it attempts to express the inconceivable in human symbols. But, taken together, these sayings of Jesus give Dominical warrant for belief in a coming of Christ *beyond history* –

> Heaven and earth will flee away,
> When he comes to reign.

This is the event which we mean by the consummation of the Kingdom.

What will it involve?

First, it must mean the final triumph of God over all the powers of evil.

Second, it must signify the point at which time – and all in history which is pleasing to God – all that the labour, service, love, devotion and suffering of man have striven through uncounted generations to effect – will be taken up into eternity.

Third, it must mean the confrontation of men by God in Christ. Here our clue to the second coming is the first one. God has already revealed himself to us in a Man from whom we may learn what sort of person it is with whom, at the last, we shall have to do. We shall encounter the same person whose holiness, compassion and love are known to us from the Gospels.

It is the teaching of Jesus, as it is of his apostles, that it will involve *judgment* – a sifting of good from evil: not perhaps the legal proceedings on a cosmic scale which some have pictured so much as the finalizing, in another world, of verdicts already passed in this one, and indeed, as St John emphasizes (e.g. John 3.18), already passed by men on themselves.

But, equally, the consummation will mean the perfect fruition of life in the eternal world of God, the wiping away of all tears, the triumph of Christ and his saints. The supernal world will be like a feast, and life like that of the angels of God (Mark 12.25). Then the promises of the Beatitudes will come fully true: the mourners will be comforted, the pure in heart will see God 'face to face', and his redeemed children will be for ever at home in their 'Father's house' (John 14.2).

When will this consummation happen? We do not know the time, nor did the Son himself (Mark 13.32). It is a reserved secret in the breast of God. Nor is it the Christian's business to speculate on 'the day or the hour'. It has been finely said[9] that New Testament thought on the Last Things, at its deepest and best, always concentrates on what God has already done for men in Christ. It does not say, How long will it be before the final whistle blows 'full time'? Rather it says, 'Where ought I to be now to receive the next pass?' What really matters is that the kick-off has already taken place, the game is on, and we have a Captain who can lead us to victory.

[9] C. F. D. Moule, *The Birth of the New Testament*, 101f.

6

The Lord's Prayer

I

In his diary for March 1, 1939, the Scottish poet Edwin Muir described how he underwent a kind of conversion by reciting the Lord's Prayer as he took off his waistcoat. He was 'overcome with joyful surprise (he says) when he realized that everything in the Lord's Prayer, apart from the Being to which it is addressed, refers to human life, seen realistically, not mystically, and that it is about the world and society, and not about the everlasting destiny of the soul'.

It is a pity that most of us could not undergo a similar conversion and see the Lord's Prayer with new eyes, because the words are so familiar that we seldom pause to consider what they mean. I don't suppose, for example, that the average church member has many difficulties about the Prayer beyond the simple one of whether to say 'debts' or 'trespasses'. So let me dispose of this one straight away. 'Debts' is undoubtedly the Biblical word; but 'trespasses', which occurs in the Anglican *Book of Common Prayer*, has, so to speak, Dominical sanction, because at the close of the Lord's Prayer, in Matt. 6, Jesus, commenting on it, says, 'For if you forgive men their *trespasses*, your heavenly Father will also forgive you.'

This problem disposed of, let me begin by saying that we have two versions of the Lord's Prayer and that the one we use is Matthew's version. This version comes in the middle of the Sermon on the Mount, and is introduced as an example of how his disciples ought to pray: 'Pray then like this', says Jesus.

The other version you will find in the eleventh chapter of Luke. 'Lord, teach us to pray', say the disciples, 'as John (the Baptist) also taught his disciples.' Jesus replies, 'When you pray, say Father . . .', and there follows the Model Prayer.

Now if you compare the two versions in the RSV text, you will find that, if the substance of the Prayer is the same, Luke's version has seventeen words fewer and shows some verbal variations.[1] Why do we have two different versions? In answer some have suggested that they represent the teaching of Jesus given on two different occasions. Others have suggested that Matthew's version was the one used in the churches of Syria, and Luke's that current among Gentile Christians. Whatever be the truth, Matthew's version has certainly been the favourite one down the centuries, as it is undoubtedly the more satisfying.

Neither version, observe, has the familiar doxology at the end: 'For thine is the kingdom and the power and the glory for ever.' Why? Because the words do not occur in our oldest and best MSS. But if the doxology was not a part of the Prayer as Jesus taught it, we know that a doxology very like ours was attached to it by the end of the first century.[2] Jewish prayers normally ended with a doxology: in this case Jesus left it to his followers to supply the actual wording.

One more preliminary point is worth making. Nowadays the Lord's Prayer is, so to speak, common property, so that many a man, however loose he may sit to the Christian Faith and church membership, thinks he has the right, on occasion, to use it. It was not so in the earliest days. Then the Lord's Prayer, along with the Holy Supper, was reserved for members of the Church; and it was probably at their baptism that converts were first allowed to repeat it as a mark and privilege of their new status.[3] It was to this Paul probably was referring when he said, 'When we cry "Abba! Father!" it is the Spirit himself bearing witness with our spirit that we are children of God' (Rom. 8.15).

II

In what sense is the Prayer original? The question is worth asking

[1] For a discussion of these variations see my *Design for Life*, 68f. In the AV Luke's version of the Prayer has been assimilated by scribes to the more familiar one in Matthew.

[2] In the *Didache*, a short Christian manual, produced probably in Syria about AD 100.

[3] According to Tertullian, catechumens were taught the Lord's Prayer eight days after they had received the Creed.

because from time to time some Jews try to tell us that everything Jesus said is to be found either in the Old Testament or in the sayings of their rabbis. So they ransack Jewish sources to find parallels to this or that phrase in the Lord's Prayer. Thus, for example, one very old Jewish prayer has the words, 'May his great name be magnified and hallowed in the world.' Another contains the words, 'Forgive us, our Father, for we have sinned against thee.'

Such parallels should not shock or surprise us. The work of a great artist is not to manufacture his pigments but with them to paint a great picture. So Jesus, using older materials, made his perfect Prayer.

On the positive side, we may find the originality of the Prayer in:

(a) its *brevity*. Here is no 'much speaking' – no holy verbosity – but six short petitions that go arrow-like to the unseen world;

(b) its *order*. The Prayer puts first things first, the heavenly things before the earthly; and

(c) its *universality*. The Prayer is concerned wholly with the needs common to humanity, so that all men, whatever their class or colour, can make it their own. It is, as Helmut Thielicke puts it, 'the Prayer that spans the World'.

III

The *plan*, or shape, of the Prayer is simplicity itself. After the Invocation – 'our Father who art in heaven' – there follow six petitions. Three are for God's glory; three are for man's needs. First, we are to pray for God's greater glory – the hallowing of his name, the coming of his Reign, the doing of his will – then for our human wants, for what we might alliteratively call provision, pardon and protection. Note the order: first, world issues, then our human needs; and both, for Jesus, are in the hands of the great Father God who at once shapes the course of history and attends to the individual wants of his children.

Now let us consider the *name* and the *purpose* of the Prayer. We call it 'the Lord's Prayer'; and so it is, but because he taught it, not, I think, because he prayed it. We cannot imagine Jesus, who

showed no consciousness of sin, praying to be forgiven his sins –
unless of course, though himself sinless, he associated himself
with sinners even to the point of joining with them in their
prayers.

Did he then give it as a formula or as a guide? Since his command is, 'Pray then like this', the answer would seem to be, 'As a
guide'. Yet we do not use this Prayer amiss if we repeat it as we
do, provided that we try to pray it meaningfully and do not make
it just a piece of holy patter.[4]

This Prayer, then, should serve as the mould and type of all
Christian prayer. Understand this Prayer, and you understand
how every true follower of Christ ought to pray. Do you wish to
know whether you may pray for this or that thing in Jesus' name?
Then ask yourself, Can it be legitimately covered by the petitions
of the Lord's Prayer?

Now we are ready to study the Prayer phrase by phrase,
petition by petition.

IV

Look first at the Invocation: 'Our Father who art in heaven' – or,
if 'who art in heaven' suggests to any 'honest to God' Christians
'God way up there', then quite simply 'Our heavenly Father'.

The key-word here is 'Father'. As the supreme question for any
religion is, What is God like? so, for Christians, there is only one
right answer, Christ's answer: God is Father. (And, for Jesus,
observe, 'Abba, Father' was not just one more metaphor for God,
but the supreme reality of his own life, an experience of un-
paralleled intensity and depth.)

God is our heavenly Father. Not a Principle, not a Force,
but a Person, and not any kind of a Person, but a Father. It was
Jesus' way, in teaching his disciples, to say, 'Think of the very
best human father you can imagine – God is all that – and far
more.' Great beyond all our comprehending, holy beyond all our
conceiving, but a Father – a Father who cares for his children,
who is sad when they go astray, who is glad when they come home:

---

[4] Our word 'patter' meant originally to repeat the *Paternoster* and so to
gabble prayers.

the Father to whom his own life was one long and loving obedience, and to whom he committed his spirit on the Cross. This is the God we invoke as 'our Father'. Yes, mark the pronoun 'our', and note the 'us-es' that follow it: 'give us', 'forgive us', 'lead us', 'deliver us'. This is a *social* prayer. When we say, 'Our Father', we join ourselves with the whole family of God in the wide earth.

Turn now to the first petition, 'Hallowed be thy name'. Straight away it strikes the note of adoration. But observe the passive voice of the verb: 'May thy name be hallowed.' Our scholars call this a Jewish 'reverential passive'.[5] It means 'May God cause his name to be held holy'. But what is God's 'name'? We say, 'What's in a name?' as if it were merely a label devised for the postman's convenience. In the Bible, however, the 'name' stands for the person himself – for his nature and character.

Now the God whom we worship is not 'an unknown God'. He is the God who has revealed himself as holy Father. So in the first petition we pray: 'May God cause his nature as Father to be reverenced everywhere, and may men come to honour and obey him as such.'

The second petition reads: 'Thy Kingdom come'. Here the commonest mistake people make is to picture the Kingdom of God territorially, as some sort of Super Welfare State under Divine Patronage. The Kingdom, or Reign, of God is nothing of the sort. It signifies not man contriving but God acting – God acting in his royal power. It means the sovereign activity of God in saving men and overcoming evil, and the New Order of things thus established.

Now it is the very heart of the Gospel, or Good News, that this saving Rule of God really and decisively began when he sent his Son, by his life and death and resurrection, to reconcile a sinful world to himself. This, however, was only a beginning – the inauguration, not the consummation; and in his parable of The Mustard Seed Jesus said that from this unremarkable beginning would come unimaginable endings. The Kingdom, or Reign, of God then has been inaugurated; it has not been consummated. So

[5] Like 'they shall be called sons of God' in Matt. 5.9. The NEB rightly translates, 'God shall call them his sons'.

when you and I pray, 'Thy Kingdom come', we pray our heavenly Father to *complete* the great purpose of salvation which he took in hand when he sent his Son among us.

When that Kingdom comes, all evil will be abolished, and all the promises of God will come true. Then the Beatitudes will become facts: the mourners will be comforted, the pure in heart will see God face to face, and his redeemed children will be finally and for ever at home in their heavenly Father's house.

Now consider the third petition, 'Thy will be done on earth as it is in heaven'.

Only God can consummate his Reign. Does this mean that man is to sit back with folded arms and do nothing? Is it an invitation on the lines of the student's parody of the well-known hymn:

> Sit down, O men of God,
> His Kingdom he will bring
> Whenever it may please his will:
> You cannot do a thing.

No indeed! This petition reminds us that *we* have our part to play in God's great scheme. But see what we have too often done with the words! We have turned what was meant to be a battle cry into a wailing litany. We have made the words into a tombstone *cliché*, when they ought to be a summons to God's servants to be up and doing – doing God's will. 'Thy will be done – and done by me.'

What is God's will? What pleases God. And what that is Christ has told us – in the Sermon on the Mount and elsewhere. It is health, not disease; service, not selfishness; giving, not grabbing; loving, not hating; the Golden Rule, not the rule of the jungle. In God's presence it is always so; and here we pray that earth may become in this like heaven.

So the first half of the Prayer comes to an end. Having 'asked for the big things', we are now free to pray for our own needs, and, in particular, for provision, pardon and protection.

'Give us this day our daily bread'. This, the fourth petition, teaches our dependence upon God. Sometimes we say a man has 'independent means'. But nobody really has. We cannot command the harvest; God gives it. And all the tractors in the world would be so much useless metal if God did not quicken life within the seed. No, our 'daily bread' comes not from the farmer, not from the miller, not from the baker but from God. And this our dependence on him we acknowledge whenever we say 'Grace before meat'.

But notice two things: First, Jesus authorizes us to ask God only for what we need. It is a prayer for daily bread, not for cake: for the staff of life, not for luxury. Second: this petition is not an invitation to idleness. It does not rule out the human effort needed to make God's gift our own. As somebody has observed, 'God feeds the sparrows, but he doesn't put the crumbs into their mouths.'

The fifth petition is about forgiveness, human and divine: 'And forgive us our debts as we forgive our debtors.' 'Debts' mean 'sins'. There is, says Jesus, another hunger, the soul's hunger for forgiveness of all the sins that separate us from our heavenly Father; and as we all sin, we all need to ask God's forgiveness.

But mark the words he adds: 'As we forgive our debtors.' Where forgiveness is concerned,[6] we have never a simple linear relation between God and man: it is always a *triangle* – God, my neighbour and I. Our sins have repercussions on other people, as other people's sins have repercussions on us. Accordingly, any effective forgiveness must pierce the barbed-wire entanglement of human wrongs and estrangements. And if it is to do so, obviously there must be wire-cutting on *man's* side as well as on God's. In other words, the two forgivenesses go together – we cannot expect God to forgive us if we won't forgive our neighbour who has wronged us. When General Oglethorpe said to John Wesley, 'I never forgive', Wesley replied, 'Then I hope, sir, you never sin.'

The last petition reads, 'Lead us not into temptation but deliver us from evil'.[7]

It is a prayer for Divine protection in time of spiritual danger. But 'lead us not into temptation'? Is Jesus implying that God

---

[6] I owe the following illustration to T. W. Manson.

[7] So far as the Greek goes, 'deliver us from evil' might also be rendered 'deliver us from the evil one', i.e. the devil. But whether we translate 'from the devil and all his works' or 'from the evil forces in the world and the will behind them' is not a practical question of great importance.

makes men do evil? Well, the Greek word *peirasmos* can mean temptation to do wrong, but its common meaning is 'trial' or 'testing'. Here the word stands for the dangers and difficulties that confront the good man trying to do his duty to God and his neighbour. It represents all those forces which would entice or drive God's servants into disloyalty to him.[8] Is it not natural to pray to be spared these things? So the first half of the petition expresses an understandable human shrinking from 'trials' or what we might call 'moral adventures'. Now if God does not 'tempt' any man (in the sense of enticing him to do evil) he *does* permit such 'trials'; and indeed without them we would never develop any moral muscle or backbone. Therefore the whole petition means: 'Spare us, O Lord, moral and spiritual adventures, so far as may be; but when they do some, give us thy help to come victoriously through them.'

Then, as with a peal of trumpets, the Prayer ends with the ancient doxology – 'for thine is the kingdom, and the power and the glory for ever' – and we are back where we began in the thought of the majesty and perfection of God.

That is the Lord's Prayer, the *Paternoster*, the Prayer that Jesus taught his disciples, the Family Prayer, the Prayer that teaches us to pray. It is so short and simple that a child can understand enough to pray it. On the other hand, the saint or the sage can never plumb all its depths. Unfathomable? Yes, but how universal too! For, as Edwin Muir said, it is about 'the world and society', concerns itself with the needs of all men, high and humble, rich and poor, white and yellow and black.

There is just one thing more to be said. You will have noticed that, though Jesus gives us the Prayer, he is never himself mentioned in it; he seems to retire completely into the background. Nevertheless, I repeat that it is Jesus himself who gives us the prayer. It is the Lord crucified and risen who is the invisible background of all its petitions, our surety for its truth. For he alone, in his life, and death, and resurrection makes us sure that there is a great invisible Someone whom we can address as 'Abba,

---

[8] The story of the Temptations shows that Jesus knew how searching and severe such 'trials' can be.

Father', that this Father God is at work in this sinful world building his Kingdom of mercy in the secrecy of the Cross, that God hears his children when they cry to him in their need, and that, come what will, all evil will finally be defeated and God be all in all.

'When you pray, say, Father . . . thy Kingdom come.' This is the Prayer Christ gave his disciples nineteen hundred years ago. It is still the Prayer of every true Christian, the Prayer which he ought to pray every day – every day and with 'all that in him is'.

7

The Sermon on the Mount

After nineteen hundred years the Sermon on the Mount still haunts men. They may praise it, as the great Indian Gandhi did; or they may curse it, as the German philosopher Nietzsche did. Ignore it they cannot. Its words are winged words, quick and powerful to rebuke, to challenge, to inspire. And though some recoil from it in despair, it continues, like some great magnetic mountain, to attract to itself the greatest spirits of our race, so that if some world-wide vote were taken, there is little doubt men would acclaim it the greatest utterance on the moral life we possess.

Sometimes in history men have almost forgotten it or, perhaps deliberately, in time of war, have put it in cold storage. But always it has leapt again to life; and when human society falls on evil days and moral decay sets in, men return to it wistfully, half persuaded that in its 107 verses is the cure for all our moral and spiritual ills.

Sometimes men talk as if the Sermon on the Mount were all plain sailing: a collection of practical rules for everyday living. All we need to do, they suggest, is to write the teaching of Jesus in the Sermon into the statute books of the nations, and we shall have a blue-print for some kind of heaven on earth. It is then that others arise to ask, Is the Sermon indeed all plain sailing? And is it a morality for all men? So the debate goes on. Some would persuade us that the heart of the Gospel is contained in the Sermon, as though the Cross and the Resurrection were irrelevancies. Others, with a much better understanding of the New Testament, are quite sure that the heart of the Good News is something God has *done* for man, and not simply something God *demands* of men.

What is the truth about the Sermon? Three questions call for answers. (1) What is the Sermon's place in the Christian scheme of things ? (2) Was it meant for the followers of Jesus or for all men – for the Church or for the world at large ? (3) Did Jesus intend it to be a new Law as binding on his followers – the New Israel – as the Law of Moses had been binding on Old Israel ? And, over and above all these, is the question of the Sermon's relevance and importance today for us, who live in other days and other climes, and are vexed by other problems, social, national and international ?

These are our main questions. But, first, we must say a word on the making of the Sermon.

I

The Sermon, the first of five great discourses in his Gospel, is to be found in Matthew, chapters 5-7. (A much shorter version is to be found in Luke 6.30-49.) St Matthew introduces it thus:

> When he saw the crowds he went up the hill. There he took his seat, and when his disciples had gathered round him he began to address them (NEB).

The ordinary church member, reading these words, naturally supposes that Jesus delivered the ensuing 107 verses in a single, non-stop discourse, and that one of his disciples – possibly Matthew, a man of some education – made notes of it which later were incorporated in his Gospel. The truth, however, is not so simple. We need not doubt that Jesus gave this teaching to his disciples in some such setting, but we may be sure that he did not give them all this teaching 'at one fell go'. If he had, then only disciples with memories like Lord Macaulay would have remembered it all, and they would certainly have suffered from spiritual indigestion! Beyond doubt the Sermon gathers up into one splendid whole teaching given by our Lord on many occasions.

How it all originated, a knowledge of Jewish teaching techniques will help us to understand. First, the Jewish teacher would discourse to his disciples on some chosen topic; then he would sum up his instructions in a few pointed and pregnant sentences or maxims; and finally he would go over these with his disciples again and again till they had them by heart. We have good reason to believe that the greatest Teacher of all did exactly this. But he did more. Everybody knows that poetry is easier to memorize than prose – for an example, we need think only of our rhyme for remembering the months of the year, 'Thirty days hath September, etc.'. Now a study of the form of the Sermon will show that our Lord cast a great deal of it in couplets and even stanzas,[1] so that it might stick in his disciples' memories. Even in an English translation this poetic style comes through, and makes it unforgettable.[2]

Such then were the Galilean beginnings of the Sermon. So, in the quiet teaching-sessions of a busy Ministry when the disciples went to school with Jesus, he gave them a pattern for living as God meant men to live. How all this teaching of Jesus came to be recorded in writing and gathered together in the masterly discourse which St Augustine was the first to name 'the Sermon on the Mount', is a long and rather complicated story, involving discussion of Gospel sources.[3] I will not weary you with it now: enough to say that the present shape of the Sermon suggests that the evangelist had the needs of new converts in view when he set down Christ's teaching on paper. To the first disciples, who by obeying his call had entered the Kingdom of God, Jesus had sought to show how God meant men to live. What more natural than that later apostles and church leaders, wishing to set before their converts the moral ideal to which Christ called them, should have gathered together the Sayings of Jesus, as Matthew has done, to serve as design for living in that New Era which had dawned on the world with the Resurrection of Christ and the gift of the Holy Spirit?

II

From the making of the Sermon let us turn now to the matter. Beginning with Beatitudes and ending with the parable of the Two Builders, it has six main themes: (1) the kind of people God takes pleasure in; (2) the righteousness he demands; (3) the worship he rewards; (4) the service he requires; (5) the faith to which he calls; and (6) the treatment he would have us show to others.

[1] See, e.g. the words beginning, 'Ask, and it shall be given you.'
[2] The classic discussion of this subject is C. F. Burney's *The Poetry of our Lord*.   [3] See my *Design for Life*, 13f.

Rightly do the Beatitudes, or 'Blessed Sayings', stand first, for they are the very soul of the Sermon. In these tremendous paradoxes Jesus describes the kind of people God takes pleasure in – the truly blessed ones. Eight times he turns the world's notions of blessedness upside down. Who are the people the world counts fortunate? Is it not the rich, the gifted, the successful, the famous. Yet not a single one of these figures in Christ's bede-roll of the blessed. No, it is 'the poor in spirit' (those who know their spiritual inadequacy before God), the mourners, the humble, those who long to see right prevail, the compassionate, the pure-hearted, the peace-makers, and all persecuted for righteousness's sake – on these God's benediction rests. These are the heirs of his Kingdom: these will find mercy, be comforted, see God, be called his sons, and win a heavenly reward.

What is the role of such men in the world? They are to be the salt which keeps society from corruption, the light which will illuminate a dark world (5.3-16).

The next theme is the higher righteousness. 'I have not come', says Jesus, 'to destroy the law and the prophets. I have come to bring out the full meaning of the old revelation and complete it.' You remember (he says) how the old Law prohibited this act and that, prescribing due penalties for offenders. But I tell you, God's will and interest are in the hidden springs of conduct, where the writ of law does not run at all:

If the old Law said, No murder, I say, No anger.
If the old Law said, No adultery, I say, No lust.
If the old Law said, Divorce on condition, I say, No divorce.
If the old Law said, No false swearing, I say, No swearing at all.
If the old Law said, An eye for an eye, I say, No retaliation.
If the old Law said, Love your neighbour, I say, Love your enemy (5.17-48).

If in these six antitheses Jesus were promulgating a new code of laws, we might well despair. No anger, no lust, no retaliation – what man among us can rise to the height of these demands? If Jesus meant these as new laws on the perfect keeping of which our salvation depended, who could be saved? But neither here nor elsewhere in the Sermon does Jesus appear in the role of legislator: he is declaring the pure will of God, enunciating God's moral ideal for us men. How far we fall short of it, we know only too well in our hearts. More clearly than any other section of the Sermon these six antitheses indict us all as sinners. We may give thanks with St Paul that we are saved not by law but by God's grace.

From the new righteousness Jesus turns to the worship God desires. 'Be careful', he warns, 'not to make a show of your religion before men.' He singles out three aspects of man's approach to God – almsgiving, prayer and fasting – and in each example hammers the same point home. All piety done to purchase human applause has no reward with God. What matters before all else is secrecy and sincerity – sincerity before God who sees what is done in secret and rewards it. Therefore, when you do some act of charity, no publicity; when you pray, no 'playing to the gallery' while you profess to be seeking God's presence; when you fast, your contrite heart should be for God's eyes alone. Only this is worship in spirit and in truth (6.1-18).

From the worship God desires the Sermon proceeds to the service he requires. First Jesus dwells on treasures – earthly and heavenly: store up, he says, heavenly ones – the only ones that last. Then in the little parables of the Single Eye and the Single Service he calls for undivided allegiance to God: 'You cannot be a slave to both God and Mammon' (6.19-24).

Service to God leads Jesus naturally on to speak of *faith*. His disciples must learn to worry less about material things and to trust God more. Let them study the wild birds and the wild lilies – those lilies today in bloom with a glory transcending Solomon's, and tomorrow dead and gone. It is an old motif this of the transience of life – 'the grass withers, the flower fades' – but Jesus gives it a quite new turn. His point is not, 'These pass, and so must you.' It is: 'You see how much care God lavishes on birds and lilies, ephemeral though they are; how much more will he care for his children!' So the sovereign cure for anxiety about material things is a greater faith in a heavenly Father who knows all his children's needs before they ask. Let his disciples seek first God's sovereignty and all else will be theirs (6.25-34).

The last theme of the Sermon is the treatment of others.[4] As God will be your judge, says Jesus, you must be slow to search out the faults of your neighbours. Never take the splinter from your brother's eye till you have removed the plank from your own. And in dealing with your fellow-man let your golden rule be to treat him as you would have him treat yourself (7.1-12).

The Sermon is ended. What remains is a call to decision and a challenge to action. As trees are to be recognized by their fruits, so they must make their deeds match their professions. On Judgment Day pious words by themselves will be of no avail. In all times of crisis and at the last great Crisis the secret of security will be a life founded on deeds done to the divine design he has given them (7.13-28).

III

From the making of the Sermon, and its matter, we now turn to its *meaning*. How is it to be interpreted?

Obviously, the Sermon deals with character and conduct and falls into the category of what we call ethics. What kind of ethic do we find in the Sermon? The short answer is that it is *an ethic of grace*.

If you are to understand any famous words rightly, you must take them in their original context, set them against the background in which they were originally uttered. Thus, you will never understand Winston Churchill's 'I offer you blood, tears, toil and sweat' till you remember 1940 and the mortal danger in which this nation then stood. Just so you will never begin to understand Jesus' sayings in the Sermon till you set them against the background of that supreme crisis in the ways of God with men – the coming of the Reign of God – which was the burden of all our Lord's words and works. The Gospel which Jesus came proclaiming was that a new chapter in the story of God's dealings with men was opening – that the Reign of God was dawning – that God, taking the great initiative, was breaking graciously into history to visit and redeem his people. It was the Good News of the beginning of God's new Era of grace, his almighty love going

---

[4] Matt. 7.7-11 are about *prayer* – compare Luke 11.9-13.

into action to save undeserving men, his free gift of forgiveness and eternal life to all who would, by repentance and faith, accept it.

This is the true setting, context, background – call it what you will – of all that Jesus says in the Sermon, from the Beatitudes to the Golden Rule. What we have in the Sermon is an outline, a sketch, a design of the kind of conduct and behaviour expected in all who have closed with God's offer of grace which has come with the coming of Christ and the Kingdom.

If then in the Sermon Jesus says to his disciples, 'You must forgive others', it is because they themselves have already received the assurance, 'Your sins are forgiven'. If he calls them to be 'the light of the world', it is because they have already found in him 'the light of the world'. If he bids them live as sons of God, it is because they already know themselves to be children of Abba, Father. If he calls them to 'love their enemies', behind Jesus' command lies the dynamic of the boundless love and grace of God. In fact, all the things Jesus calls for, all the kinds of action he demands, all the patterns of behaviour he desiderates, are but samples, and illustrations, of the kind of moral fruit to be produced in lives that have been transformed by the grace of God. In every instance in the Sermon the gift of God – his grace – precedes the demand. It is a case of 'Freely you have received: therefore freely give'.

We are now able to answer the three questions raised at the beginning.

To the question, What is the place of the Sermon in the Christian scheme of things ?, the answer is: The Sermon is not the Gospel, but its corollary.

Go back to the first days of the Church. For the first Christians the Gospel was not the Sermon on the Mount but the Cross on the Hill and the Empty Tomb. In the mission and message of Jesus the Messiah, in his death on the Cross for men's sins, in his triumph over death and in the gift of the Holy Spirit, they said that God had manifested his saving Rule, and men must know about it, and accept it as true if they were to be saved. The Gospel was the Good News of something God had *done*, not of something that He *demanded*. It is still so.

But this Good News has a corollary – a consequence for conduct. Since the Kingdom of God has come in Christ (though it is not yet consummated) – since it has created a new community, a Church, living under that Rule – it follows that believers in Christ must live in a Kingdom Way.[5] That Kingdom Way the Sermon describes. It tells how men ought to live who have experienced this grace of God in Christ.

The second question was: Is the Sermon intended for the Church or for the world at large? Again the answer has been emerging by implication as we went along. All the teaching in the Sermon is *disciple-teaching*. It is not for all and sundry, but for those who, by following Jesus, have entered the Kingdom of God. P. T. Forsyth[6] put it thus: 'It is an ethic of the Kingdom, and it is only for the world as it comes to seek first the Kingdom of God.' When Jesus spoke the Sermon, it was to committed men. It remains so still. It is a Dominical pattern of life for all who take Christian discipleship seriously, for all who truly confess Christ as Saviour and Lord.

Third question: Did Jesus intend the Sermon to be some kind of new Law – a code of commandments which must be perfectly kept and fulfilled if a man was to be saved?

If that were true, then Jesus who called men weighed down by the Law to come to him and find 'relief',[7] was laying on his followers far heavier burdens than the scribes and Pharisees did on theirs.[8] This is patently absurd. No, if one thing is clear, it is that Christ is no legislator riveting on his disciples a new code of laws, to be literally and legally enforced. What Jesus is enunciating in the Sermon is the principles of action that ought to govern men's lives in that new order of grace which is another name for the Kingdom of God. What he gave his first followers – what he still gives his followers today, is direction, not directions, a design, and not a code.

---

[5] The early Christians were known as followers of 'the Way' (Acts 9.2, 19.9, 24.14, etc.).

[6] *The Expositor*, 1915, p. 128.   [7] Matt. 11.28.   [8] Matt. 23.4.

IV

How far can the Sermon give us guidance for Christian living today? This is our final question.

'All this Sermon on the Mount business', says one of Rose Macaulay's characters, 'is most saddening, because it's about impossibilities. You can receive a sacrament, and you can find salvation, but you can't live the Sermon on the Mount.'

But can Christians thus dodge the issue by saying that the Sermon is 'about impossibilities'? After all, we have been at pains to show that Christ does set before his followers a real design for living, and not merely a counsel of perfection. He tells us what kind of people God takes pleasure in; what kind of personal and social behaviour God wills for his children; what kind of worship God rewards; what kind of service God requires of us; what kind of faith he calls us to; and what kind of treatment he would have us show to others. And, as Dr Joad once said, most of us know in our hearts that 'Christ's prescription for living is the right prescription'.

Relevant then in this sense, the objector may say, but is the Sermon really practicable? Can it be lived?

Two extreme answers to this question have been given, both of them, I believe, misguided.

Some Christians have seen in the Sermon 'a terrifying summons to repentance', and held that Christ meant it to be such. The Sermon (they say) shows us how far we 'come short of the glory of God', exposes us as sinners and so casts us on the Cross which is God's remedy for sin. Well, no question at all that the Sermon does convict us of our sin by showing us how God means us to live. But we may be sure that Jesus never *meant* it as a kind of 'frame up' to ensure the failure of us all and so bring us to the Mercy Seat for mercy.

At the other end of the scale, some Christians have held that the Sermon is a collection of straightforward precepts which admit of easy practice. How misleading this view is an appeal to experience will show. What man, even the best of us, does in fact live his life according to the pattern laid down in the Sermon? Who keeps himself quite free from anger, or hate, or impure thoughts ? Who forgives without reservation ? Who loves without a limit ? Who trusts God with a faith unshadowed by any hint of anxiety ? The answer is, No one.

Yet, it must be insisted, Christ meant his teaching to be a pattern for real living, not a blue-print for Utopia. Listen to him: 'Whosoever hears these words of mine and acts on them . . .' and, again, 'Why do you call me Lord, Lord, and do not the things I say ?' Further, we must never forget that we are not asked to scale the heights of the Sermon in our own unaided strength. On the contrary, we are offered the continuing help of a living Lord who comes to us now through the Holy Spirit and has promised to be with us 'to the end of time'.[9] And this living Christ, as T. W. Manson[10] picturesquely put it, still has two hands – one to point the way, the other held out to help us along.

In that assurance we Christians today can face the heights and challenges of the Sermon. And beyond any doubt, if we will but use it, the Sermon does give us stimulus and guidance for Christian living. In any given moral dilemma the Christian may ask himself, 'What light and leading may I derive from the principles and precepts of my Lord as I know them from the Sermon ?' The Sermon is not an ordnance map, giving detailed ethical information for our guidance; but it most certainly is a compass, Christ's compass which will give us moral bearings. If it does not give us cut-and-dried directions, it most surely gives us direction – God's direction. Do not we Christians today need just such stimulus and direction ?

To be sure, the ethical heights of the Sermon will always be beyond us. But is not this as it should be ? As Browning put it,

> A man's reach should exceed his grasp,
> Or what's a heaven for ?

No man, this side of eternity, measures up to the Sermon's standards. We judge ourselves by them, and know that we are sinners. Yet if none of us ever attains the mountain-peaks to which Christ summons us, this but illustrates the tension between the ideal and the actual which must for ever mark the lives of

---

[9] Matt. 28.20. NEB.   [10] *Ethics and the Gospel*, 68.

Christ's followers in this world. For we have to live our lives at once as citizens of this world, with all its trials and temptations, and as citizens of 'a commonwealth' which, as Paul said,[11] 'is in heaven'. Thus, though we no more than the first disciples can ever hope in this world to achieve the ideal, we are called on, day by day, with our Lord's help, to keep striving towards it. For it is design for life in the Kingdom of God.

[11] Phil. 3.20 RSV.

8

The Miracles of Jesus

The miracle stories in the Gospels are either lies, or legends, or history. If all, or most of them, are lies or legends, the claim which Christianity has been making for well-nigh two thousand years, is false. But is it?

C. S. Lewis[1] makes this interesting remark about miracles: 'God does not shake miracles into nature at random as from a pepper caster. They come on great occasions; they are found at the great ganglions of history.' Such a 'great ganglion of history' was the Ministry of Jesus; indeed, in his own view, it was the greatest of all the ganglions. If Lewis is right, the story of Jesus ought to contain miracles, as indeed it does. But we are running ahead too fast, for we must first ask, What do we mean by miracles? When we have done this, we may then go on to ask what place they have in the Ministry of Jesus, and whether they are credible by Christians today.

Miracles, then, we may define as extraordinary interventions of God in history, not necessarily breaches of natural law, but unusual enough to draw attention to themselves. Let this serve as a working definition, for we are not primarily concerned with the question whether Jesus wrought miracles in the sense in which this or that philosopher used the word (say, David Hume). As ordinary Christians we are interested in the question whether Jesus healed the sick, stilled the storm and raised the dead.

And the short answer is that, unless the Gospels are a tissue of lies, Jesus did perform miracles of this kind. According to the Gospels, Jesus wrought many wonderful cures on men's bodies and souls, and exercised on occasion an extraordinary power over what we call 'inanimate nature'. These acts of extraordinary power are called in the first three Gospels 'mighty works'

[1] *Miracles*, 201.

(*dunameis*: lit. 'acts of power'), and in the fourth, 'signs', i.e. significant acts which are revelations to faith.

The next point to note is that miracles bulk very large in the Gospels, and that we find the miraculous element in the Gospel tradition as far back as we can go. Thus in Mark, the earliest of the Gospels, no less than 209 verses out of a total 661 – that is, 31% – deal with miracle.[2] In short, the story of Jesus was told from the beginning as that of one who worked miracles. Miracles, then, are not late importings into the story of Jesus; they are part of the primary stratum. We can no more eliminate them from the Gospels than we can eliminate the water-mark from a sheet of good note-paper.

But if the miracles are woven into the warp and woof of the Gospel record, what is their place and purpose in the story?

I

Down the centuries men have thought very differently about Jesus' miracles. For a very long time they believed that the purpose of the miracles was *evidential*. They were proofs of the heavenly origin of Jesus. They served as seals which accredited him as the divine Son of God. This was the view, for example, of William Paley in his famous eighteenth-century book entitled *The Evidences of Christianity*. Nevertheless, it is open to two fatal objections. First, Jesus did not work miracles in order to call attention to his credentials. The narrative of the Temptation (Matt. 4.1-11) shows that, right from the beginning, Jesus resolved that God's Messiah should not indulge in what we might call 'stunts' in order to win a following. Later in his Ministry he steadfastly refused the Pharisees' request for a 'sign', or legitimating proof, of his divine authority. 'No sign', he said, 'shall be given this generation' (Mark 8.12). In the second place, this evidential concept of miracle does violence, as we shall see presently, to the close connexion between miracle and faith. In short, the whole picture of Jesus as a kind of heavenly bellman summoning men to believe in his divinity through his miracles is quite out of keeping and character in one of whom it was said, 'He

[2] A. Richardson, *The Miracle Stories of the Gospels*, 36.

shall not strive nor cry, neither shall any man hear his voice in the streets' (Matt. 12.19).

Very different from the evidential view was the attitude to Jesus' miracles adopted in the nineteenth century by Liberal Protestants like Matthew Arnold. It was a time, let us recall, when science seemed to be explaining everything and to be revealing a universe which was one vast closed system of cause and effect. In such a universe miracles appeared as violations of the uniform order of nature – arbitrary intrusions into this great closed system. Not surprisingly, many concluded that miracles were therefore impossible and dismissed the mighty works of Jesus as later and legendary accretions to the Gospel story.

The only trouble about this view is that it blandly assumes the answer to the one question that really matters: Is nature really a closed system, quite impervious to invasions from Super-nature – from God? This, as we shall see, is a quite unproved assumption. The mischief really started, T. W. Manson said, when the working hypotheses of natural science were allowed to become the dogmas of Protestant theology.

Meanwhile we must say that neither the evidential nor the Liberal view of miracle will do. The miracles of Jesus are not seals attached to the document, but part of the document itself. They are not, as the Liberals often said, a semi-legendary frame to be discarded; they are part of the picture itself.

How then are the miracles regarded in the Gospels themselves? It is here that modern scholarship has recovered for us the true view.

The whole burden of Jesus' preaching was the Kingdom, or Reign, of God. Now the Kingdom of God means the sovereign activity of God in saving men and overcoming evil, and the New Order of things thus established. Moreover, it was the very heart of Jesus' 'good news' that this New Order had begun in his mission and message. For him the mighty works were signs, for those who had eyes to see, of the Kingdom's presence and power. They were tokens of that New Order in which the power of the living God was at work through his Messiah in hitherto unknown ways – encountering and defeating evil, whether it was the demonic distortion of men's personality, the assault of disease on his natural vigour and vitality, or the foretaste of death. In short, the miracles of Jesus were the Kingdom of God in action, not an extra but an integral part of his message. If by word and parable he announced the advent of the Kingdom, his 'mighty works' were signs for the spiritually percipient that God's saving Rule was among them. 'If I by the finger of God cast out demons,' he said, 'then is the Kingdom of God come upon you' (Luke 11.20; Matt. 12.28).

It is but another side of the same medal when we note that Jesus saw his miracles as the fulfilment of the prophets' predictions concerning the Messianic Age. Thus when the Baptist sent from prison to ask, 'Are you the one who is to come (i.e. the Messiah), or shall we look for another?', Jesus' reply was in effect, 'You remember what Isaiah prophesied about blind men receiving their sight, deaf men hearing, lame men walking and dead men being raised up? Well, these things are happening now in my ministry. Draw your own conclusions' (See Matt. 11.5ff.). In the same vein he said to his disciples, 'Blessed are the eyes that see what you see. For I tell you that many prophets and kings desired to see what you see and did not see it, and to hear what you hear, and did not hear it' (Luke 10.23f.).

II

If, then, the miracles of Jesus are tokens of the coming of the Kingdom, let us study their characteristics.

Regarding them from the human angle, we note first the stress Jesus sets on the need for *faith*. Faith in Jesus' God-given power to heal is the pre-condition of his miracles; and where such faith is wanting, as it was at Nazareth (Mark 6.5), miracles are not easily wrought. We need not quote all Jesus' demands for faith; but notice the demand that Jesus often makes for the patient's active co-operation in a cure. 'Have you the will to health?' he asks the cripple at the Pool of Bethesda (John 5.6). Elsewhere his commands to the sick and diseased are invitations to co-operate in the divine work he is doing. 'Rise, pick up your bed and walk.' 'Stretch out your hand.' 'Go and wash in the pool of Siloam.' Or, again, observe the sheer pertinacity of the people who seek a cure either for themselves or those they represent: the paralytic's friends who took down a bit of the roof in order to get him into Jesus' presence, the woman with the hemorrhage resolved at any cost to touch even the hem of his garment, blind Bartimaeus who refused to be silenced by the bystanders. In all these cases faith is no mere pale, passive belief; it is 'the energetic and importunate grasping after God's help' present in Jesus.

Along with this note the stress Jesus sets on prayer (which is really faith in action). We moderns, half-hypnotized by the apparently 'steel-and-concrete' order of nature, ask timidly, 'What may we pray for?' Jesus has no such inhibitions. 'I tell you,' he says, 'whatever you ask in prayer, believe that you receive it, and you will' (Mark 11.24). We wonder whether we may pray for material blessings. Jesus in his pattern prayer for his disciples includes a petition for 'daily bread'. Clearly he believed in the power of prayer to influence the circumstances of life, and he saw his miracles as divine answers to his prayers.

But faith and prayer are only one half – the human half – of the secret of his miracles. What of the divine side? 'By the finger of God' is Jesus' own answer (Luke 11.20. The parallel in Matt. 12.28 has 'Spirit'). He regards his miracles as tokens of God's Spirit working in all its fulness through himself.

At his Baptism Jesus knew himself to be 'the anointed of the Spirit'. Whatever else this meant, it meant equipment with divine power. Except on this assumption, the ensuing temptations in the wilderness become pointless and unreal. His words in the synagogue at Nazareth carry the same implication. 'The Spirit of the Lord is upon me', he says, quoting Isa. 61, 'because he has anointed me to preach good news to the poor. He has sent me to proclaim release to the captives and recovering of sight to the blind' (Luke 4.18). Jesus therefore regarded not only his preaching of the 'good news' to 'the poor', but also his conquest of disease and the devil as inspired by God's Spirit. His 'acts of power' represented the energizing of God's Spirit through himself to save sick and sinful men and women. 'The Father who dwells in me', Jesus says in John's Gospel (John 14.10), 'does his works.'

III

We come last to the credibility of his miracles. Can a modern Christian who values his intellectual honesty accept them?

Before we answer this question, two important things need to be said.

First, and granting the possibility of miracle, we must in every case be satisfied that there is good evidence for any particular miracle. After all, on any definition of it, a miracle is a highly unusual event. It requires good evidence. (Thus we should need only slight evidence if a man told us that he had once seen King George the Sixth riding in Windsor Great Park. But we would require overwhelming evidence if someone told us he had seen Charles the First riding in the Park with his head underneath his arm!)

Moreover, to be good evidence, it must be early evidence, evidence not too far removed from the event. If we use this criterion, obviously some of Jesus' miracles are better attested than others. For example, the healing of the Officer's Son, which occurs not only in Matthew and Luke but also in the independent Gospel of John, is better attested than the turning of Water into Wine which occurs only in John. Furthermore, doubt about any particular miracle does not of course discredit the lot.

The second point to remember is this: the miracles of Jesus were performed among a people who had no doctrine of 'secondary causes' and therefore sought a supernatural explanation for any event that baffled popular understanding. Jesus' contemporaries were a bit like the pious lady in Defoe's book who, on seeing a bottle of over-ripe beer explode and fly in froth to the ceiling exclaimed, 'O the wonders of Omnipotent Power!' Nowadays we have a chemical explanation for the explosion. The point is that we who have a better understanding of such 'secondary causes' are entitled, to that extent, to 'rationalize' the miracles, always provided that our 'rationalization' does not caricature the historical evidence. Thus, if Mark 15.33 tells us that at the time of the crucifixion 'darkness fell over the whole land' from noon till three in the afternoon, we are not required to postulate a supernatural phenomenon such as superstitious fancy associates with the death of great men –

> When beggars die, there are no comets seen,
> The heavens themselves blaze forth the death of princes.

A black Sirocco wind laden with thick dust from the Judean desert is the natural and likely explanation.

With these two provisos, we may now return to the matter of credibility.

First, it is true to say that Jesus' *healing* miracles should impose no strain at all on a Christian's faith. We are beginning to realize that man is 'psychosomatic' and to recognize the potent part played by the mind in the cause and cure of disease. (Even the layman knows that worry can cause stomach ulcers, and some doctors have cured warts by suggestion.) We all know something of the achievements of modern psychotherapy. And there is the evidence of spiritual healing, to be found in books like Cameron Peddie's *The Forgotten Talent*. All these things conspire to bring Christ's healing miracles within the range, if not of our powers, at least of our belief. True, we cannot match the speed of his cures, neither can we heal at a distance. But if, to put it at its lowest, we remember the extraordinary personality of Jesus, we shall wisely refuse to say we will accept only those healing miracles which we, with our present knowledge, can effect. And the secret of the cures at a distance – the Officer's Son and the Syro-Phoenician Woman's Daughter – is surely to be sought in the person of Jesus and the divine answers to his prayers.

Ultimately it is the *nature* miracles – the Feeding of the Multitude, the Stilling of the Storm and the Walking on the Water – which modern men find hard to believe. Here we may try rationalization. Thus it may be that the Feeding was a great open-air sacrament – Jesus' parable of the Great Supper (Luke 14.16-24) acted out, at which he gave everyone present a morsel of bread in token that those who had shared his table in obscurity would one day share it in his glory. It may be, as St John implies,[3] that Jesus

---

[3] 'In John there is no miracle whatever' (J. H. Bernard, *St John*, 185). 'It is the recognition of Jesus, unexpectedly present to the disciples in their need, that is the true centre of the story' (C. H. Dodd, *Historical Tradition in the Fourth Gospel*, 198).

was walking by the Lake shore, not in the middle of it, when suddenly, as by a miracle, he loomed out of the storm and darkness to reassure his terrified disciples. And it may be that what Jesus stilled was not the storm on the Lake but the storm of fear in the disciples' hearts.

The first two suggestions, in my judgment, contain truth. The third is an obvious caricature of the evidence. Rationalizations of this last kind always leave us with the feeling that if this was all that happened, the story would never have been told. In the last resort, therefore, our verdict on such miracles will depend on two things.

The first is our *world-view*. Here it must be allowed that the last half-century has seen a remarkable change. Gone are the days when scientists could dogmatically declare that miracles, because they were 'violations of the laws of nature', were therefore impossible. The so-called 'laws of nature' are now seen to be simply convenient summaries of existing knowledge which have always to be revised in the light of later research; and the discoveries of the last few decades – wireless waves, the splitting of the atom and so on – have shown that reality as perceived by us is by no means identical with reality in itself. Modern scientists are therefore readier to confess ignorance in the face of ultimate mysteries, and to allow that there are far more things in heaven and earth than their predecessors were prepared to admit.

This brings us to the second and – for the Christian – the quite fundamental thing: our *estimate of Jesus*. All turns on what we think of him. If a man can see in him only a prophet, then, while he may accept the healing miracles, he will probably reject the nature ones. But if Jesus was, and is, what Christians have always believed him to be, the Son of God in a lonely and unshared sense, if in him the Spirit of God was uniquely incarnated, if his will was completely synonymous with the Divine will, there is nothing inherently incredible in the belief that such a person as Jesus may have had control over the great frame of nature itself.

In a word, grant 'the grand miracle' of the Incarnation, grant that God became man in Jesus, and most of the objections to his miracles fall to the ground.

The Christian philosopher T. E. Jessop[4] has put the issue in one sentence:

If the universe is dominated by a Spirit, miracles are possible; if by a Spirit that is love, probable; and if that Spirit has become incarnate this miracle would make further ones very probable indeed.

With the help of modern scholars we have been studying the miracles of Jesus, putting them in their proper context in the Ministry, noting their characteristics, even allowing that here and there the miraculous element may have been heightened in their telling and re-telling. But we have not been eliminating miracle from the Gospel record.

I began by saying that miracle belongs to the very stuff of the Gospel tradition. Let me end by saying that all those who want a Christianity without miracle are in peril of relapsing from true Christianity into mere 'religion'. By 'religion' I mean the watered-down, nebulous version of the Faith which often passes for Christianity today – the kind of crypto-pantheism which is a 'hangover' from the teaching of men like Hegel and Wordsworth. The Deity in this 'religion' is a God who, as Carlyle once complained to Froude, 'does nothing' and therefore no miracle. Such a God who wills nothing, does nothing, demands nothing, who is 'only there if you ask for him like a book on the shelf', is not the living God of the Bible or of authentic Christianity. Most certainly he is not the God and Father of Jesus, or the God who raised him from the dead, of the apostles' preaching. The God of Jesus, the Christian God, is pre-eminently 'the God who acts', the Divine Workman whose workshop is history. He is the God who delivered Israel from Pharaoh's hosts at the Red Sea, who took Christ from the tomb and gave him the highest place that heaven affords, and who poured out his Holy Spirit on his first followers at Pentecost. For such a God the Divine art of miracle is not the art of suspending the regular pattern of events or of breaching the so-called 'laws of nature'; his is the art of feeding new and extraordinary events into the pattern of history of which he is Lord, of intervening sovereignly in that order of nature which is his creation. He is the God both of nature and of grace, whose mighty acts are

[4] *The Christian Faith*, 18.

still to be seen by men of faith not only in the returning snowdrops and the recurrent miracle of the Spring but also in 'the great ganglions of history', the God who is shaping its course, in ways past our human understanding, to that blessed pattern and end revealed to us, once for all, in Jesus Christ his Son.

9

The Parables of Jesus

The first three Gospels contain some sixty parables, the fourth perhaps a dozen. How do you conceive of them?

When I was young, I used to think of them as pleasant stories with morals attached, improving tales suitable for children in Sunday School. Now, years later, many of these same parables seem to me more like Churchill's speeches in 1940 – weapons of war in a great campaign against the kingdom of evil, a campaign which took Jesus to the Cross. This is the measure of 'the new look' that has been coming over the parables in our time, so that we now understand them better than any Christians since the apostolic age.

But this is to anticipate conclusions: we had better begin at the beginning.

In Sunday School we were taught to define a parable as 'an earthly story with a heavenly meaning'. This is true enough, so far as it goes. Rather different is the definition given by one of P. G. Wodehouse's characters. 'A parable', he says, 'is one of those stories in the Bible which sounds at first like a pleasant yarn, but keeps something up its sleeve which suddenly pops up and leaves you flat.' True, again. Lots of parables contain 'the ambush of the unexpected'. Nathan's parable of the little ewe lamb (II Sam. 12.1-4), with its final 'Thou art the man!', certainly left King David flat.

However, to please the pundits, we had better be a little more precise. The word parable, Greek in origin, means a 'comparison'. We may therefore define a parable as a comparison, drawn from nature or from daily life, and designed to teach some spiritual truth, on the assumption that what is valid in one sphere – nature or daily life – is also valid in the spiritual world.

The next point is that parable is a form of *teaching*. Dean Inge has said, 'Almost all teaching consists in comparing the unknown with the known, the strange with the familiar.' It is a matter of everyday experience that you cannot explain anything except by saying that it is *like* something else, something more familiar. So the Gospel parable often begins, 'The Kingdom of God is like . . . like leaven . . . or like a mustard seed – or like a drag net.' Only notice that you cannot stop there. The Kingdom of God is not like leaven, but like what happens when you put leaven into a batch of meal – a heaving, panting mass, all motion, bubbles and energy.

Combine, then, this method of teaching by analogy with the Oriental's liking for pictorial speech and Everyman's love of a good story, and you have most of the reasons why men took to using parable, in order to convey truth.

Parables, of course, are found in the Old Testament as well as in the New. Notice also that the Hebrew word for parable, *mashal*, is a wide label for all kinds of figurative speech – from a simple metaphor to an elaborate story. So it is with the Gospel parable. 'Physician, heal thyself' is a parable (Luke 4.23), though it has only three words; but so also is the Prodigal Son, which has nearly four hundred.

At its simplest, therefore, a parable is a figurative saying, sometimes a simile like 'Be ye wise as serpents', sometimes a metaphor like 'Beware of the leaven of the Pharisees'. What you and I know as parables are simply expansions of these. 'All we like sheep have gone astray' is a simile. Expand it into a *picture*, and you get what is called a 'similitude', e.g. the parable of the Lost Sheep. Expand it into a *story* by using past tenses, and you get a story-parable like The Great Supper.

Our Gospel parables are mostly either similitudes or story-parables. The difference is this. The similitude describes some common, everyday process – like putting a patch on a coat or yeast into meal, whereas the story-parable describes not what men commonly do but what one man did:

> A sower went forth to sow.
> A certain man made a great supper.

What, then, is the difference between parables and allegories? Although one or two of Jesus' parables come close to being allegories, most of them are not. The chief difference to grasp is that in an allegory, like *The Pilgrim's Progress*, each detail in the story has its counterpart in the meaning. By contrast, in a parable, e.g. The Unjust Steward, story and meaning meet not at every point but at one central point (in this case the Steward's 'gumption' in a crisis). In other words the allegory has to be de-coded point by point like a crossword puzzle. In the parable proper there is one chief point of likeness between the story and its meaning; and the details simply make the story more realistic and serve the main thrust of the parable, like the feathers which wing the arrow.

The other difference is this: the true parable must be realistic, life-like – must 'hold the mirror up to nature'. By contrast the allegory need not obey the law of life-likeness, but may stray away into some 'Never-Never Land', as many of them do.

Now, with these distinctions drawn, I want you to notice three features of our Lord's parables.

First: they follow the rules of popular story-telling. Down the centuries men have found that stories are told more effectively if you follow certain rough rules. One is 'the rule of contrast', whereby virtue and vice, wisdom and folly, riches and poverty are contrasted. Gospel examples are The Wise and Foolish Maidens and The Rich Man (Dives) and Lazarus. Another is 'the rule of three', whereby your story has three chief characters ('An Englishman, an Irishman and a Scotsman . . .'). Gospel examples are the three travellers in the tale of The Good Samaritan and the three excuse-makers in The Great Supper. And a third is 'the rule of end stress', whereby the spotlight falls on the last person or act in the series – whether it is the youngest son or the final adventure. Think for example of the 'barren rascal' in The Talents who did nothing with the money entrusted to him, or the sending of the only son in The Wicked Vinedressers.

The second point is that Jesus' parables were extemporized in living encounter with men rather than slowly elaborated like sermons in ministers' studies. For Jesus' parables arise out of 'real life' situations, and are often 'weapons of war' in his long controversy with the Pharisees. Thus the three great parables in Luke 15 – The Lost Sheep, The Lost Coin and The Lost Son – were all ripostes to Pharisees who had criticized Jesus for consorting with publicans and sinners.

The third point follows from this. Every parable was meant to 'strike for a verdict' or to evoke a response in action. 'What do you think?', Jesus often begins a parable; and where the actual words are wanting, they are implied. 'He who has ears to hear, let him hear', he often concludes. This means: 'What you have heard is more than a pleasant story. Go and work it out for yourselves.'

All I have been saying paves the way for the question, Why did Jesus use parables?

The short answer is: to quicken understanding by putting truth in a vivid way and to challenge men to action. The parable says 'See, judge, act'. Yet we must also recognize that the Gospel parable is not always clear as daylight nor is it meant to be. It is designed to make people think – even think furiously – and to act. Seen thus, the parable is not to be confused with the 'illustration' in a modern sermon, which so often serves as sugar-coating for the theological pill. The parable is not a crutch for limping intellects; it is a spur to spiritual perception: and mostly it challenges to action – is existential.

From the question why let us turn now to the question where? Where did Jesus get the stuff of his parables?

The short answer is: from the real world all around him, the world of nature and of human nature. As Sir Edwin Arnold said:

> The simplest sights we met:
> The sower flinging seeds on loam and rock;
> The darnel in the wheat; the mustard tree
> That hath its seed so little, and its boughs
> Wide-spreading; and the wandering sheep; and nets
> Shot in the wimpling waters – drawing forth
> Great fish and small – these and a hundred such
> Seen by us daily, never seen aright,
> Were pictures for him from the book of life,
> Teaching by parable.

Even larger in the parables bulks 'the human situation' and the lives of ordinary men and women in home, or farm, or market. The

Leaven goes back to the time when Jesus watched 'Mary his mother' hiding the yeast in three measures of meal, The Splinter and the Plank to the Nazareth workshop. The parable of The Playing Children,

We piped for you and you would not dance.
We wept and wailed, and you would not mourn. (Matt. 11.17 NEB)

takes us back to a Nazareth street where the lads and lasses 'made believe' at weddings or at funerals. (It was the boys who played at weddings, the girls at funerals.) Then as now there were labourers who hung about in the market place 'because no man had hired them'. Probably the Galilee of Jesus' day knew a rascally 'factor' (steward) who was the original of The Unjust Steward. And so on.

(In all this one thing is clear. Jesus believed that human life with all its faults and frailties could furnish pointers to the Kingdom of God, and that our human care and concern could figure forth the care and concern of the Almighty Father.)

One final question. Can we be sure that we have the parables substantially as Jesus told them?

The answer is Yes, and for various good reasons. For one thing, in many parables the background is authentically Palestinian. In The Sower, for example, sowing precedes ploughing, as it still does in Palestine today. If 'we plough the fields and scatter', they scatter and plough the fields. For a second point, the parables reveal Jesus' highly individual way of speaking and thinking – the daring faith in God (e.g. in his parables on prayer), the swift surprises of thought so characteristic of him, the many flashes of hyperbole and humour which we know were his. And for a third and more general consideration, it is worth noting that great parables are evidently so hard to create that it is difficult to name another person in history with more than one or two good ones to his credit.

We may therefore be quite sure that in the parables we are in direct contact with the mind of Jesus.

Nevertheless, one change the parables did undergo in the thirty or forty years that elapsed between Jesus' speaking of them and the time when they were written down in our Gospels. In the time of what is called 'the oral tradition', when as yet there was no New Testament and the Christian message was passed from mouth to mouth, the parables took on a new lease of life as the apostles and early Christian preachers used them in their preaching and teaching; and inevitably they re-employed and re-applied them to their own situation and that of their hearers. Thus the parable of The Lost Sheep which Jesus originally addressed to the Pharisees and which spoke of the redemptive joy of God at a sinner's repentance, became, in the early preachers' use of it, a summons to pastoral concern for lapsing church members. (See Matt. 18.12ff.) It is important to remember this use of the parables by early preachers when we come to enquire into the original thrust of the parables as Jesus told them. Some people are disconcerted to learn that the early preachers thus re-applied the Lord's parables to fit their own situation. But why should we fault the early Christians for doing this when similar things are done every Sunday (and rightly) from Christian pulpits today?

Now let us say a word about how the parables have been interpreted by Christians down nineteen centuries. You remember I began by saying that we now understand them better than most of our Christian predecessors. Let me explain.

In the early Christian centuries the Church Fathers tended to treat the parables as allegories. In the allegory each detail of the story is a separate metaphor with a meaning of its own which has to be discovered. By contrast the parable enforces one main point, and the rest is realistic trimming. Thus the parable of The Prodigal Son proclaims one sovereign truth – the free forgiveness of God to penitent sinners. But note what happened when the early Church Father Tertullian got busy expounding it. The elder son in the story is the Jew; the younger, the Christian. The patrimony of which the younger son claimed his share is that knowledge of God which a man has by his birthright. The citizen in the far country to whom he hired himself is the devil. The robe given to the returning prodigal is that sonship which Adam lost at the Fall. The ring is the sign and seal of baptism; the feast is the Lord's Supper; and who is the fatted calf slain for the feast but the Saviour himself?

Well, that kind of allegorizing persisted in the Church for nearly eighteen centuries; indeed, it still persists in some quarters. There is, however, really no excuse for it, because thanks to modern scholarship we now know better.

Towards the end of the nineteenth century a German scholar named Jülicher proved that, by and large, the parables are not allegories, to be spelled out point by point, like a crossword puzzle. On the contrary, they exist mostly to make one point; and the details are but the feathers which wing the parabolic arrow to its mark. But if the parables exist to make one point, what kind of point is it? It was here that Jülicher, having rightly insisted on the one point, went on, Irishly enough, to miss it. His capital mistake was to make the parables teach moral commonplaces, or truisms. Thus, for Jülicher, the meaning of The Talents is, 'A reward is only earned by performance'; and of The Unjust Steward, 'Wise use of the present time is the condition of future happiness'. But was Jesus really this kind of person? Did he go about Galilee pointing morals for the multitudes by means of picturesque stories? Would men ever have bothered to crucify a preacher of prudential platitudes? Of course they wouldn't!

But if Jülicher had left his task half done, he had paved the way to that true understanding of the parables which we owe to two great living scholars, C. H. Dodd and Joachim Jeremias. What then did they do that Jülicher had not done?

The answer is: they put the parables of Jesus back into their true historical setting, which is the Ministry of Jesus seen as the great act of God in which he visited and redeemed his People.

But are not the parables already in that setting? Many are but some are not: You will recall that the early preachers took the Lord's parables and re-applied them to suit their own situation. Once you realize this, you can begin to restore these re-applied parables to their original setting. What is it?

All the parables of Jesus have to do with the coming of the Kingdom of God. To understand what this means, you must remember that for centuries the Jews had been praying for the time when the God of heaven would really take to himself his great power and reign. Now it was the very heart of Jesus' 'good news' that this blessed time was no longer a shining hope on the far horizon but a dawning reality. The arm of the Lord was being revealed; God was really beginning to reign. And, as you read the Gospels, you begin to see that the whole Ministry of Jesus – his preaching, teaching and healing – is in fact the inauguration of that Kingdom, God acting in his royal power, God vanquishing the forces of evil that hold men in thrall.

This is the true background of all Jesus' parables – the great campaign of the Kingdom of God, with Jesus as its spearhead, against the kingdom of evil; and once you understand it, you can see how all the parables fall into their proper historical setting, and become pregnant with point.

I propose now to arrange the chief parables in four groups, each of them illustrating some aspect of the Kingdom of God.

1. First, *the Coming of the Kingdom.*

Four parables tell how the Kingdom comes and grows: with certainty and to great and unimaginable endings, say the two parables of The Mustard Seed and The Leaven. Quietly but nevertheless irresistibly, says the story of The Seed growing secretly. And, in spite of all failures, yielding a bumper harvest,[1] says that story of a farmer's fortunes which we call The Sower. But Jesus does not confine himself to images from agriculture. He sees the Kingdom of God as a Great Supper to which the invitation goes out, 'Come, for all things are now ready', or as a Drag Net which catches all sorts of fish.

2. The second group of parables may be entitled *the Grace of the Kingdom.*

'Grace' is God's extravagant goodness to undeserving men, and in all the parables of this group this is the dominant theme. Take the Labourers in the Vineyard (or, as it might better be called, The Good Employer). In that tale Jesus is saying, 'The rewards of the Kingdom are not to be measured by men's deserts but by God's goodness.' This in answer to the Pharisees who had criticized Jesus for offering the blessings of the Kingdom to tax-

---

[1] 'Thirtyfold, sixtyfold, and a hundredfold' (Mark 4.8). Tenfold was reckoned a good harvest in Palestine.

collectors and harlots. For the strange thing is that all these parables of Grace were spoken to his critics in defence of his 'good news'. All three parables in Luke 15 – The Lost Sheep, The Lost Coin and The Lost Son – say in effect, 'If a man will be at such pains to recover his lost property, how much more does God desire to save his lost children! This is what the Almighty is like, and this is why I, as his Agent, act as I do.'

3. The third group of parables describes *the Men of the Kingdom*.

To be a disciple of Jesus is to be 'in the Kingdom', since Jesus himself embodies and is the Kingdom. The parables in this group all suggest the meaning of true discipleship. Before men decide to follow Jesus, they must 'count the cost', say the twin parables of The Tower Builder and The Warring King. But to win its riches is worth any sacrifice, say the parables of The Hidden Treasure and The Costly Pearl. In the stories of The Importunate Widow and The Friend at Midnight, Jesus calls for a faith which refuses to take No for an answer and expects great things from God. Let his disciples be known for their compassion, says the story of The Unmerciful Servant, and for their deeds rather than their fine professions, says The Two Builders.

4. Finally, we come to a very important group of parables all dealing with *the Crisis of the Kingdom*.

Here we need to remember that Jesus saw his Ministry, which was the inauguration of the Kingdom, moving to a great climax or crisis in God's dealings with his People, a crisis which would involve not only Messiah's death and victory and the rise of a new Israel, but also doom on the Jewish temple and nation. Against this background many of Jesus' parables become luminous with meaning. In some we hear him warning Israel's leaders about their unfaithful stewardship of God's revelation: such are The Savourless Salt and The Talents. In others he warns the Jewish people against the imminent time of God's visitation: such are The Weather Signs and The Rich Fool. In others he calls on Israel to repent before it is too late – one thinks of The Barren Figtree and the Story of The Defendant. And in others – like The Waiting Servants, The Burglar and The Village Maidens – Jesus seeks to alert them to the Great Emergency – God's time of destiny for his People – now upon them.

But, alas, Israel, as he said (Luke 19.41-44), 'did not know the time of her visitation' by God or 'the things that belonged to her peace', and the great drama moved inexorably to its climax.

So the Son of Man, the Speaker of the parables, and the chief Actor in the drama, marched on Jerusalem where, on an April morning in the year AD 30, the crisis culminated in a crucifixion outside the northern wall of Jerusalem. One parable, that of The Wicked Vinedressers, preserves Jesus' final appeal to the Jewish leaders. It is 'Love's last appeal' to a rebellious people. No full-length parable survives to tell how Jesus the Messiah conceived the purpose of his dying – though St John preserves a short one about The Grain of Wheat which must die if it is to bear a rich harvest. Yet three parables in miniature take us some way into the Lord's secret – I mean his three sayings about the Cup, the Baptism and the Ransom. The Messiah is drinking 'the cup our sins had mingled'; he is undergoing a baptism of blood whereby others may be cleansed; as the Servant Messiah he is giving his life as a ransom for many.

What was the sequel? Did the Day of reckoning – God's Reckoning – come for Israel? Did The Grain of Wheat which fell into the ground and died, bear much fruit? Was it given to Jesus the Servant Messiah to 'see the travail of his soul and to be satisfied'?

The Church of Christ is built on the belief that it was. 'When thou hadst overcome the sharpness of death', says the *Te Deum*, 'thou didst open the kingdom of heaven to all believers.' But this, the story of how Jesus met and vanquished 'the last enemy' and came back with unshadowed peace upon his lips, must be the subject of our final study. In it we shall examine the evidence which attests this stupendous event and which entitles us to cry with St Paul, 'Thanks be to God who giveth us the victory!'

Before we leave the parables, there is one more thing to be said. In none of the parables does Jesus make a quite explicit claim to be the Messiah. This, however, consists well with 'the Messianic Secret'. Nevertheless, his parables contain, for those who have ears to hear, *implicit* christological claims. 'Jesus hides himself behind the parables,' Ernst Fuchs[2] has said, 'they are veiled self-testimony and Jesus is the secret content.' C. W. F. Smith[3] makes the same point when he says that, whether Jesus explicitly claimed to be the Messiah or not, he said those things which none short of the Messiah had the authority to say. And Jeremias says the same thing, using Jesus' own language:

All Jesus' parables compel his hearers to define their attitude towards his person and mission. For they are full of 'the secret of the Kingdom of God' (Mark 4.11) – that is to say, the certainty that the Messianic Age is dawning. The hour of fulfilment has come; that is the keynote of them all. The strong man is disarmed, the powers of evil have to yield, the physician has come to the sick, the lepers are cleansed, the heavy burden of guilt is removed, the lost sheep is brought home, the door of the Father's house is opened, the poor and the beggars are summoned to the banquet, a master whose kindness is undeserved pays wages in full, a great joy fills all hearts. God's acceptable year has come. For there has appeared the One whose veiled majesty shines through every word and every parable – the Saviour.[4]

---

[2] *Theologische Literaturzeitung* 79 (1954), col. 345-348.
[3] *The Jesus of the Parables*, 291.   [4] *Rediscovering the Parables*, 181.

10

The Resurrection of Jesus

I

I once wrote a book entitled *The Work and Words of Jesus* whose last chapter deals with the Resurrection. When the Queen (now the Queen Mother), who had asked to see it, wrote to me, she confessed: 'I am sorry to say that I read the last chapter first, which is, I know, dreadful cheating: but it makes a wonderful and hopeful background to the rest of the book, and I do not regret it at all.

What a short time is 1900 years!

Perhaps the light of the Resurrection will yet flood the world.'

Like the Queen Mother, all Christians recognize the importance of the question of the Resurrection. In more senses than one it is crucial – involves a crux, or cross.

The Cross of Calvary is really a mighty question mark against the sky. If the story of Jesus ends there, then it is unmitigated tragedy, and there is no moral rhyme or reason in the universe. Let it be once established that the life of Jesus went out in darkness, and we might as well conclude that behind the universe there is no great and good Abba, Father, as he believed; and of Jesus on his Cross we might say, as Thomas Hardy said of Tess on the gallows, 'The President of the immortals had finished his sport with Jesus of Nazareth.'

Have you ever stopped to consider what follows 'if Easter be not true'? No man ever had a firmer conviction than the apostle Paul that it was true; but once, in I Cor. 15.12-19, he faced his readers with the awful consequences that followed if it was not.

'If Christ has not been raised,' he said, 'your faith is vain.' All that trust of yours in God's love and power is worth nothing. If God, watching Jesus die on the Cross, did nothing about it, your faith in him is an empty husk. 'If Christ has not been raised,' he went on, 'you are still in your sins.' Why? Because if the Cross was really the end for Jesus, he who was called to 'save his people from their sins' had failed in his mission. A dead Saviour cannot save you. But even this, Paul proceeded, is not all. 'If Christ has not been raised, then those also who have died in union with Christ have perished.' If Christ never rose, what hope have they? If Jesus' life ended on the Cross, then all 'the blessed departed' (as we call them) are perished as though they had never been, and 'we are of all men most miserable'. If the Resurrection is not true, faith is gone, forgiveness is gone, immortality is gone.

Paul is right. Without the Resurrection the Christian faith would be finished.

Well, true or false? This is our question: Is the Resurrection history's most influential error, or its most tremendous fact?

II

If you set out to argue the truth of the Resurrection, you cannot, in the nature of the case, hope to 'prove' it as you would prove a proposition in Euclid. What you can do is to give good reasons for the faith that is in you. And this you do by marshalling such historical evidence and personal testimony for the reality of the event that only the incurably prejudiced would reject it out of hand. So let us look first at the written, or documentary, evidence.

Every Christian is familiar with the Gospel stories of how Jesus appeared to his disciples after his crucifixion. What the average Christian does not know is that much the earliest written evidence for the Resurrection occurs not in the Gospels (which were written a generation or more after the crucifixion) but in chapter 15 of Paul's First Letter to the Corinthians. There, writing about AD 55, Paul reminds the Christians in Corinth of the 'tradition' which he had himself 'received' and passed on to them, tradition derived from the original apostles.

'I delivered unto you as of first importance', Paul writes, 'what I also received, that Christ died for our sins according to the scriptures, that he was buried, that he was raised on the third day according to the scriptures, and that he appeared to Cephas, then to the Twelve. Then he appeared to more than five hundred brethren at one time, most of whom are still alive, though some are fallen asleep. Then he appeared to James, then to all the apostles.'

'Last of all,' Paul adds, 'as to one untimely born, he appeared also to me' (I Cor. 15.3-8).

Let us begin by noting Paul's reference to the 'five hundred brethren' who had seen Jesus risen, most of whom were still alive when Paul was writing. It is as if he were saying, 'If you don't take my word, ask them. They saw him.' In other words, the tradition he quotes admits of checking and control.

The next and vitally important point is that this 'tradition' goes back not merely to AD 55 when Paul was writing, but to within half a dozen years of the crucifixion. The 'tradition' which calls Peter by his Aramaic name Cephas, contains several Jewish idioms glimmering through the Greek,[1] which strongly suggest that it originated in Jerusalem and the Mother Church there. Not only so, but the two apostles named in the 'tradition' – Peter and James, the Lord's brother – are precisely the two apostles whom Paul met when he went up to Jerusalem in AD 36, three years after his conversion (Gal. 1.18f.). From them, in all probability, Paul got this tradition about the Resurrection.

Let there be no mistake then about its value. 'It fulfils all the requirements of historical reliability', says Professor H. von Campenhausen,[2] the eminent German historian. 'Anyone who doubts it might just as well doubt everything that the New Testament contains – and more.'

Before we leave Paul and his 'tradition', notice one further point. Though the 'tradition' does not expressly mention the empty tomb, it implies it. 'Died – buried – raised' – the words are meaningless unless that which was buried was raised. And we may add that it would have conveyed nothing to Paul or the early Christians to say that it was the *spirit* of Christ which rose into new life.

---

[1] See J. Jeremias, *The Eucharistic Words of Jesus* (2nd edition), 101-103.
[2] *Tradition and Life in the Church*, 44f.

Now turn to the Gospel narratives about the empty tomb and the risen Christ. They begin with Mark's record of how, on the first Easter morning, three women who went to anoint Jesus' body, found the tomb empty, and 'a young man', sitting by it, said, 'He has risen; he is not here.' Speechless, trembling and astonished, they fled in terror . . . The last narrative in our canonical Gospels is St John's account of how the risen Lord appeared by the Lakeside in the grey of a Galilean dawn. In between we have various other narratives of Jesus appearing to his disciples – notably 'doubting Thomas' – in both Galilee and Jerusalem. How shall we judge of them as evidence?

Of the earliest one, Mark's, Professor Campenhausen[3] has this to say: 'No miracle in the strict sense is related. The story tells of a journey to the tomb which is found open and empty. It does not give the least impression of the marvellous or fantastic or of being in any way incredible.' How different, he adds, would have been any legend deliberately invented to support the preaching of Jesus' Resurrection!

Now consider St Luke's famous story of the Walk to Emmaus. Of this Malcolm Muggeridge[4] has said, 'The story is so incredibly vivid that I swear to you that no one who has tried to write can doubt its authenticity. There is something in the very language and manner of it which breathes truth.'

Of St John's story of Mary Magdalene's meeting with Jesus in the Garden, when she took him to be the gardener – the 'Rabboni' story – Professor C. H. Dodd[5] has said: 'It has something indefinably first-hand about it. It stands in any case alone. There is nothing quite like it in the Gospels. Is there anything quite like it in ancient literature?'

Narratives like these, then, inspire confidence. Only in Matthew's account of the finding of the empty tomb – with its reference to the earthquake and the angel who descended to roll back the stone – do we detect a tendency to make the miracle more miraculous[6]. For the rest, to all but the most incorrigible

---

[3] Op. cit. 59, 75.　　[4] *Another King*, 14 .　　[5] *Studies in the Gospels*, 20.
[6] Likewise, Matthew's stories of the guards at the tomb and the fraud of the Jewish authorities (Matt. 27.62-66, 28.11-15) read like Christian answers to Jewish allegations that Jesus' disciples had stolen his body.

sceptic, they make their own appeal. We feel we are reading fact, not fiction.

It hardly needs saying that all these stories cannot be woven into a perfect harmony without discrepancies. If they had been, we might well be suspicious. The very discrepancies that exist, so far from discrediting the narratives, show that no pious harmonizer has been at work on them; and (as anybody knows who has listened to witnesses in a law court) discrepancies in several accounts of an event are very far from proving that the event did not happen. (Thus, to take an example, there are startling discrepancies in the accounts of Waterloo as given by Wellington, Marshal Ney and Napoleon; yet nobody in his senses dreams of denying that a great battle was fought there.)

What conclusions then may we draw from the documentary evidence? On two main points we find agreement:

1. The tomb was empty. Paul implies this. The four evangelists declare it. The silence of the Jews confirms it. 'We cannot, in my opinion,' says Professor Campenhausen[7] 'shake the story of the empty tomb and its early discovery. There is much that tells in its favour, and nothing definite or significant against it. It is therefore probably historical.'

2. The resurrection occurred 'on the third day', and Jesus appeared to many of his followers, both men and women, and spoke with them on this and succeeding days.

Fidelity to the evidence requires therefore that we begin from the empty tomb. The theory that the body of Jesus was somehow spirited away from the tomb is frankly incredible. Had the Romans or the Jews removed it secretly, it would have been easy to refute the Christian claim that Jesus had risen by producing his dead body. We may be sure that they did not because they could not. Equally incredible is the theory that the disciples hid the body and then went forth to declare that Jesus had risen. Even a Jew like Klausner[8] admits this: the nineteen hundred years' faith (he says) is not founded on fraud.

If then we accept the fact of the empty tomb, as I think we

[7] *Op. cit.* 77. [8] *Jesus of Nazareth*, 359.

must, one of two explanations is open to us. Either, we say that Jesus was resuscitated from the grave in his former body – in which case we have to face the question of what happened to it after 'the forty days'. Or, we may agree with a long line of Christians beginning with St Paul, that the physical body of Jesus was transformed in the grave into 'a spiritual body' – a body no longer completely subject to the limitations of time and space, a body suited to the conditions of the higher world as our flesh-and-blood body is suited to the conditions of this one.

Notice how the evangelists agree about the nature of the Lord's risen body. On the one hand, what they tell us suggests something unearthly – Jesus can come and go through closed doors. On the other hand, his risen body retains some earthly features, since Jesus is said to have eaten and allowed himself to be handled. This suggests that, in trying to fathom the mystery of the first Easter day, we should think of something essentially other-worldly – a piece of heavenly reality – invading this world of time and sense. We are concerned with an unmistakably divine event which yet occurred in this world of ours on an April morning in AD 30 when Pontius Pilate was Roman governor of Judea.

There we may wisely leave the matter. For the chief thing in the Resurrection narratives is the disciples' invincible conviction that their Master had conquered death. Only on the basis of that conviction can we explain the amazing change that came over them in a brief time: before the Resurrection like frightened sheep, after it as bold as lions. For such an effect there is but one adequate cause – experience of the living Christ. Only thus can we explain the converting and convincing power of the message they went forth to proclaim. Only so can we explain the conviction of fellowship with a living Lord which has been the nerve of Christianity for almost two thousand years. From Paul of Tarsus and Savonarola and Samuel Rutherfurd to David Livingstone and R. W. Dale and Charles Raven there have been unnumbered men and women to cry, in the face of all doubters and sceptics, 'I *know* that my Redeemer liveth.'

There are, in fact, three great witnesses to the reality of the Resurrection:

First, the Lord's Day. No Christian Jew would have changed the sacred day from Sabbath (i.e. Saturday) to 'the first day of the week' (i.e. Sunday) except for the reason that on this day Jesus was first seen victorious over death.

Second, the New Testament. Who would have troubled to write these twenty-seven books if Jesus had ended his career as a crucified revolutionary? Every written record about him was made by men who believed in a risen Christ.

Third, the Christian Church. If the crucifixion had ended the disciples' fellowship with Jesus, it is hard to see how the Church could ever have come into existence, and harder still to explain how it has lasted nineteen centuries.

Once in King's College Chapel, Aberdeen, I remember Sir Thomas Taylor putting this argument with unforgettable force:

We live in a real world, not in a fairy tale, and in the real world you can argue back from effects to causes. Water does not rise above the level of its own source; when a tidal wave strikes the shore, we can guess at the power of the disturbance that started it on its course. We do this because the real world is a rational order in which great effects require the existence of commensurate causes. Now the Church and the New Testament rest absolutely and entirely on the Resurrection of Jesus. If there had not been men who would say, 'We have seen the Lord', and whose lives had been transformed thereby, it is certain that the Christian way of life and the Christian Church would never have existed. What kind of event brought them into existence? What kind of upheaval started that tidal wave?'[9]

That is the kind of question which, it seems to me, admits of only one right answer, the Christian one.

III

We started from the cruciality of the Resurrection; we went on to marshal the evidence for its truth. Now, finally, let us consider its significance for Christianity and for ourselves.

It has been well said that the Cross and the Resurrection are but two aspects of one great redeeming act of God, the second of which illuminates, as with a shaft of light, the first. Easter is the interpretation of Good Friday. But how?

[9] *Where one Man stands*, 66f.

To begin with, the Resurrection meant *the vindication of righteousness*, God's righteousness.

Here (to put it in the lowest terms) was a Man with an unclouded vision of moral truth, a Man who not only trusted God completely but 'hazarded all at a clap' upon his faith in him. He made the final experiment of faith – *experimentum crucis*. If that life went out in darkness, then there is no gracious God and no justice at the heart of things. The New Testament speaks far otherwise. It declares that when Jesus laid down his life on God, Nature rang and echoed to his venture of faith: God raised him from the dead, vindicated his faith, and, in vindicating him, vindicated his own righteousness.

Next: the Resurrection meant *the ongoing Ministry*. During his earthly life Jesus had described his blood-baptism, that is, his death, as a means of initiation into a fuller and freer activity, as though visualizing a time when he would be 'let loose in the earth where neither Roman nor Jew could stop his truth'. (See Luke 12.49f.). And, as a mere matter of history, so it proved to be. If we ask what precisely Caiaphas, Pilate and the rest of them were trying to do on the first Good Friday, the plain answer is that they were trying to *stop* the Ministry of Jesus. Now, in the story of the wonderful sequel, this or that detail may be doubtful, but one thing is quite certain: the Ministry of Jesus was not stopped. On the contrary, it went on and went forward – forward into Judea and Samaria, and ultimately to the ends of the earth. St Luke was right when he summarized all that led up to the Resurrection in the words 'All that Jesus *began* to do and to teach' (Acts 1.1). Nineteen hundred years later his Ministry still goes on.

And, lastly, the Resurrection meant *the defeat of death*. Jesus Christ, says the New Testament, 'has broken the power of death and brought life and immortality to light through the Gospel' (2 Tim. 1.10 NEB). But how? Does not the Great Reaper still take his grim and universal toll? And still, though Christ be risen from the dead, do not men and women pay the last debt to nature, as they have done since time began? How can Christians claim that

> Death's flood hath lost its chill
> Since Jesus crossed the River?

Let us go back to the New Testament. The first Christians did not regard Jesus' Resurrection as a dramatic verification of the truth that the dead 'live on' – one more stone, so to speak, added to the cairn of proof for the immortality of the soul. They saw the Resurrection as a *break-through* of God's eternal order into this world of sin and death. Let me take an illustration. My colleague David Cairns has recalled his thrill at listening in Normandy, one moonlight night more than twenty years ago, to a wireless message about the progress of the battle. 'Advanced elements of allied armour', the message ran, 'have penetrated the enemy forces in depth and are racing unimpeded across the open plains towards Paris.' Just so the first Christians conceived of Christ's Resurrection. The immemorial entail of death had been broken: the banners of the Prince of Life were going forward: the Kingdom of Heaven was being opened to all believers.

Christ had left one gaping tomb in the wide graveyard of the world, and his break-through – his victory over death – like the breaching of a North Sea dyke, was an event of apparently small importance whose consequences were yet incalculable. If one, and that one he who carried in his own person the whole destiny of God's People, had exploded the myth of death's invincibility, there was life – new, divine life – in prospect for all who were his. With this fatal breach made in death's dark dominion, life with the tang of eternity about it was possible, even now, for all who were in fellowship with the Prince of Life, and with it went the promise of a life hereafter as immortal as Christ's own. 'He rose,' they said, 'and we shall rise, and when we do, we shall be like him' (I John 3.2). Not a mere spiritual survival, not a crudely materialist resuscitation – 'a resurrection of relics' – but a complete transformation, with our lowly bodies changed to resemble Christ's body of glory (Phil. 3.21).

'What is sown is mortal', said St Paul, pointing the contrast between what we now are and what we shall be –

> What is sown is mortal,
> What rises is immortal:
> Sown inglorious,
> It rises in glory:

> Sown in weakness,
> It rises in power:
> Sown an animal body
> It rises a spiritual body (I Cor. 15.42-44 Moffatt).

Such was, such is, the Christian Hope.

'Only one life', said James Denney,[10] 'has ever won the victory over death: only one life ever can win it – the kind which was in Christ, which is in him, which he shares with all those whom faith makes one with him. That is our hope, to be really members of Christ, living with a life which comes from God and has already vanquished death.'

No better example of this hope can be found than Dietrich Bonhoeffer, greatest of modern martyrs, whose books are now being read the world over. Imprisoned by Hitler, he was executed by the Black Guards on April 8, 1945. Before he was led out to execution he spoke to his fellow prisoners of his hope, using St Peter's words about 'the living hope' which God has given us by raising Jesus from the dead. As his guards were about to remove him, he sent a last note to his friend G. A. K. Bell, Bishop of Chichester: 'This is the end,' he said, 'but, for me, the beginning of life.'

It is thus that every true Christian might hope to face 'the last enemy':

> Jesus lives! Thy terrors now
> Can, O death, no more appal us.
> Jesus lives! By this we know
> Thou, O grave, canst not enthral us.
> Hallelujah!

---

[10] *The Way Everlasting*, 188.

PART THREE

The Old Quest and the New

11

The Quest of the Historical Jesus

Our point of view in the previous chapters has been that of British critical orthodoxy. Now we must say something about what has been happening in New Testament studies elsewhere, particularly in Germany which, for nearly two centuries, has been the acknowledged centre of scientific New Testament research, and has specially occupied itself with what is known in scholarly circles as 'the quest of the historical Jesus'.[1]

Here in Britain, if our scholars have not so adventurously pioneered research into this or that area of the Gospels as their German counterparts, they have done solid and admirable work in various fields (e.g. the New Testament text, Synoptic studies, and the interpretation of the Fourth Gospel), and have kept the middle road of moderation and common sense, avoiding the extremes and excesses of many Germans. The fact remains, however, that, if the long debate about the Jesus of history has taken new and often stimulating turns, most of them have begun in Germany, and it is there, at the present time, that a group of scholars are now engaged in what has been called 'a new quest'.

But if we are to understand the new quest, we must begin with the old one.

I

The Original Quest

Towards the close of the eighteenth century a German rationalist named Reimarus raised the cry 'Back from the Christ of dogma to the real Jesus!' It was our duty, he said, to get back to Jesus as he really was before the Church had smothered him in its dogma. So

[1] James M. Robinson, *A New Quest of the Historical Jesus* (1959).

began the quest

> To pierce through the creeds, his features scan,
> And see him as he really is

which continued right through the nineteenth century, was temporarily halted during the first half of the twentieth, and is now proceeding again.

The nineteenth century saw the rise of the so-called 'Liberal' School. Anti-dogmatic and humanitarian in temper, they eagerly welcomed the new light being thrown on the Gospels by the young science of Biblical Criticism. Of the many 'Lives' of Jesus which they wrote two achieved notoriety. The first by D. F. Strauss, in 1835, dissolved most of the Gospel story into myth and legend and loosed a great controversy. An even greater one followed the publication in 1863 of the Frenchman Renan's *Life of Jesus*. Renan, who 'cared more for beauty than for truth', romanticized Jesus. The picture he painted was of the amiable Carpenter of Galilee who, after charming his hearers with his winsome words about God's Fatherhood and man's brotherhood, later turned apocalyptist and marched on Jerusalem to his martyrdom. Not surprisingly, 'whoever wore a cassock and could wield a pen charged against Renan'.

There were, of course, many more German Liberal 'Lives' of Jesus which, if less radical or romantic, took as their theme, 'Jesus divinest when thou most art man'. In other words, 'they were eager to picture him as truly and purely human, to strip from him the robes of splendour with which he had been apparelled, and clothe him once more with the coarse garments in which he had walked in Galilee'.[2]

Here two British books deserve mention. In his *Ecce Homo* (1865) J. R. Seeley, deliberately missing out the 'theology', painted an attractive picture of Jesus as a moral reformer. No less appealing, half a century later, was the stress on the real manhood of Jesus in T. R. Glover's *The Jesus of History*.

With the benefit of hindsight, we can now see that the sins of these Liberal scholars were mostly sins of omission.

If they did not eliminate the miracles altogether, they played

[2] *The Quest of the Historical Jesus*, 4f.

down the miraculous element, until the miracles became mere *parerga*, and not integral parts of Jesus' mission and message.

They tended to ignore the Old Testament clues to the understanding of Jesus' person and work, although his whole ministry was set against an Old Testament background.

They got the central concept of the Gospels – the Kingdom of God – all wrong, interpreting it as an inner kingdom of values, or some kind of earthly Utopia to be built on the teaching of Jesus, when in fact Jesus understood it eschatologically, as the arm of the Lord being finally and decisively laid bare for the salvation of his People.

The thoughts of the Liberal scholars about Jesus were all too human. They scaled down the imperial mind of Christ to the level of a well-meaning Sunday School teacher. Their Jesus, in short, was not nearly big enough to explain Christianity. 'Why any man should have troubled to crucify the Christ of Liberal Protestantism', said William Temple,[3] 'has always been a mystery.'

But all this was to be changed by a young Alsatian scholar's book which first appeared in an English translation in 1910. His name, now world famous, was Albert Schweitzer, his book *The Quest of the Historical Jesus*. This is a brilliant survey of the chief German attempts to tell the story of Jesus; and it writes them off, one and all, as failures: failures, because their writers, with generous doses of psychology and imagination, had produced a Jesus after their own image and ideals, a good nineteenth-century liberal humanist with a simple faith in a paternal deity.

At the end of his book Schweitzer gave us his own account of Jesus. Resolved to restore him to the world of his own time, Schweitzer found the key to Jesus' mission and message in Jewish apocalyptic. Convinced that he was the Messiah, Jesus proclaimed the cataclysmic imminence of the supernatural Kingdom of God. At first he believed it would supervene before his 'apostles' returned from their mission (Matt. 10.23). When it did not arrive, Jesus marched on Jerusalem, believing that his 'ransom' death would force God to bring this Kingdom to pass. So he threw himself on the great wheel of history, hoping it would

[3] *Readings in St John's Gospel*, xxix.

turn. But turn it did not; and we are left with the picture of the immeasurably great man hanging – deluded, defeated, dead – on his Cross.

If Schweitzer had pronounced the funeral oration of all the Liberal 'Lives' of Jesus, he had left as his own contribution a version of Jesus' story which is at once uncritical and unacceptable. Yet Schweitzer had done one very significant thing. He had raised afresh and in challenging fashion a problem which the Liberals had burked – the problem of the eschatological sayings of Jesus, notably those which concern the Kingdom of God and the Son of Man (see, for example, Matt. 10.23; Mark 1.15, 9.1, and 14.62). In the years that followed this problem was constantly to be in the minds of scholars; and it is now agreed that an eschatological interpretation of the Kingdom of God, which was the burden of all Jesus' words and works, holds the true key to his story.

If we ask what difference an eschatological reading of the Gospels makes, we may answer in F. R. Barry's words:[4]

> The whole story moves in an atmosphere of wonder, fringed, as it were, with a numinous corona, whose flames leap up in immeasurable splendour into spaces which we cannot chart. We cannot tear it out of that setting. Apart from it there is no story to tell. And it is the triumph of the eschatologists to have recovered that atmosphere.

II

From Schweitzer to Bultmann

Had the whole quest ended in utter failure? In the half-century following it certainly looked like it. The flow of 'Lives' of Jesus seemed to come to a standstill. If we ask why, part of the answer is that scholars were wrestling with the problem Schweitzer had left them – the eschatological sayings in the Gospels – and trying to find better solutions to it than he had.

But there was another reason. The early 'twenties' witnessed the beginning in Germany of 'Form Criticism' in which K. L. Schmidt, Martin Dibelius and Rudolf Bultmann were the pioneers. The findings of the first Form Critics seemed to render the quest

[4] *The Relevance of Christianity*, 98.

well nigh impossible. The Liberals had based their 'Lives' of Jesus on the framework of the Ministry provided in Mark's Gospel. Schmidt affirmed that we could not trust it because it was of Mark's own inventing. The more radical Bultmann found that the Gospels were written in the light of the Easter faith and were so shot through with the beliefs of the early Church that they could no longer be regarded as reliable sources for the historical Jesus.

Forty years have gone by since the Form Critics startled the world of New Testament scholarship with their sceptical conclusions, and we are now able to see the weaknesses of the Form Critical method and the quandary of German historical scepticism in a truer light. Nevertheless, in the years before the Second World War, the findings of Bultmann and his colleagues had their inevitable effect: men were so impressed, or rather depressed, by them, that few were brave enough to try again to tell the Story of stories to dying men.

Nor did our neo-orthodox theologians, Barth and Brunner, who arose about the same time as the Form Critics, encourage the resumption of the quest. Indeed, they told us it was not really necessary. To busy oneself with the problem of the Jesus of history was (they implied) a denial of the nature of true faith. To try to prove that Jesus is the redemptive act of God by historical research, is to seek a false security, for true faith is essentially a kind of leap in the dark. Barth and Brunner, indeed, tried to disengage Christian faith from the relativities of history, and looked around for a sphere of 'super-history'[5] (*Heilsgeschichte* as compared with *Weltgeschichte*) or of existential encounter in which the salvation events may have taken place.

So we come to Bultmann, who has dominated the theological scene in Germany for the last generation as truly as Barth dominated the one before it. For most students his name stands for three things: (i) the radical Gospel criticism of which we have spoken; (ii) demythologizing the New Testament; and (iii)

---

[5] A history beyond the range of the bullets of the 'positivist' historians, i.e. the so-called 'scientific' historians whose main quest was for 'bare facts' and cause-effect relations, and who had no place for 'acts of God' in their scheme of things.

existentialism as expounded by his former colleague in Marburg, Martin Heidegger.

What does Bultmann think of the quest of the historical Jesus and its importance for Christian faith?

The Gospels are palimpsests in which the faith of the early Church has been so heavily written over the tradition about Jesus that 'we can now know almost nothing concerning the life and personality of Jesus'.[6] What we can trace behind our 'kerygmatized' Gospels is a non-Messianic prophet who called men to decision in face of the imminent coming of the Kingdom of God. This prophet really has no relevance for Christian faith. To understand Jesus, Bultmann says, all that is necessary is to proclaim that he has come. Accordingly in his *Theology of the New Testament* he devotes only thirty pages to the Jesus of history and describes him as 'a presupposition for the theology of the New Testament rather than a part of the theology itself'.[7]

For Bultmann the *kerygma* – the proclamation of the mighty acts of God in Cross and Resurrection – is the thing. He writes:[8]

Christ meets us in the preaching as one crucified and risen. He meets us in the word of preaching and nowhere else. The faith of Easter is just this – faith in the word of preaching.

It would be wrong at this point to raise again the problem of how this preaching arose historically, as though that could vindicate its truth. That would be to tie our faith in the word of God to the results of historical research. The word of preaching confronts us as the word of God. It is not for us to question its credentials.

The real Christ, then, for Bultmann, is the preached Christ; and when he is truly proclaimed today, God in Christ confronts men with his presence and challenge and calls on them for decision – decision for life or death – or, rather, as Bultmann significantly phrases it, for 'authentic' or 'inauthentic' existence. Here we detect the influence of Heidegger's philosophy as expounded in his *Being and Time*; and we may appropriately turn now to Bultmann's second major contribution to New Testament studies – his proposal to demythologize the Gospel.

Study the New Testament, he says, and you will find that not only its whole picture of the world – its cosmology – but its very

---

[6] *Jesus and the Word*, 8.   [7] Vol. I, 3.   [8] *Kerygma and Myth*, 41.

formulation of Christian faith is pervaded by first-century mythology which means nothing to modern man as it stands. Belief in a three-storeyed universe, in nature miracles, in angels and demons at war in the world plus the whole doctrine, in Paul and John, of a pre-existent Christ who comes down from heaven, gives his life as a sacrifice for sins, is raised by God from the dead and exalted to his right hand 'whence he will come in glory to judge the quick and the dead' – all this, Bultmann says, is first-century mythology and starkly incredible to men accustomed to use electric light and think in scientific thought-forms.

Shall we then dismiss the Gospel as a bunch of exploded myths? No, says Bultmann, myths are the deepest clue to history because they are the ancient way of describing human existence; and the Gospel can still be made relevant for modern man if we will take the trouble to re-interpret its mythology in terms of Heidegger's philosophy of Being. Here is a philosophical cradle in which Christ and New Testament theology can be laid, without adulterating its essential message and with the hope of making it speak to man's condition today.

But is Heidegger's philosophy, which is very doubtfully theistic, the kindly cradle for the Gospel which Bultmann supposes? Some of those who have studied it have grave doubts. 'Heidegger – Cuckoo or Cradle?' asks David Cairns,[9] and answers by declaring that it is a cuckoo which, unless summarily dealt with, will shoulder the Christian chicks from the nest. If we take Bultmann's line about Jesus, we may end up with 'a twentieth-century existentialist, a kind of pre-existent Heidegger'. So wrote T. W. Manson,[10] who also said, 'Bultmann promises to give us Christianity without tears. What he gives us is tears without Christianity.'

Such then was the pass – or *impasse* – to which radical German theology seemed to have come by the time of the Second World War. The quest for the historical Jesus is well-nigh hopeless; but it does not greatly matter, since the Jesus of history is largely irrelevant for Christian faith today. But we still have the New

9 *A Gospel without Myth?*, Ch. 2.
10 *The Background and Eschatology of the New Testament*, 20.

Testament *kerygma* to preach. To be sure, it is mythological; but with Heidegger's help, we can re-interpret it for modern man. The forgiveness of sins can be preached as man's deliverance from his past, from 'inauthentic existence';[11] faith can be reconstructed as 'open-ness to the future'; and salvation can be proclaimed as liberation into 'authentic existence'. Man can save himself if only he will make the right decision. To your pulpits then, you preachers, and to your existentialist *kerygma*!

The whole Bultmannian proposal is open, however, to one quite fatal objection. For Bultmann, as his former pupil Bornkamm[12] says, 'Jesus Christ has become a mere saving event and ceases to be a person.' What is the use of a *kerygma* in which the central figure is only a faceless eschatological event? How can this 'mere saving event' which is no longer a person, master me and summon me to decision?

III

The so-called New Quest

Shortly after the Second World War the untenability of Bultmann's position seems to have dawned on some of his old students, now themselves professors. There began what the American scholar James M. Robinson has called 'a new quest of the historical Jesus'. It might more accurately be called a process of Bultmannian 'revisionism'.

Ernst Käsemann started it in 1953.[13] If, he argued, we separate off the authentic sayings of Jesus in the Gospels from those elements derived from the early Church or from Judaism, we can know something about the Jesus of history. A study of these sayings will show that, though Jesus spoke of his divine mission rather than his person, what was implicit in his teaching was correctly interpreted by his apostles when they preached him as

---

[11] For Heidegger, 'inauthentic existence' is that determined by the pressures of society and convention. 'Authentic existence' is freedom to become our true selves by opening ourselves to the possibilities of Being (God?). See J. Macquarrie's *Martin Heidegger* (in the 'Makers of Modern Theology' series).

[12] *Kerygma and History* (Ed. Braaten and Harrisville), 186.

[13] *Essays on New Testament Themes*, 15-47.

the Messiah and Son of God. There is a real connexion between the historical Jesus and the *kerygma* of the early Church.

Taking their cue from Käsemann, Günther Bornkamm[14] and Ernst Fuchs[15] carried the new quest a stage further. Bornkamm dwelt mainly on Jesus' *words* and the unique note of authority to be heard in them. Jesus, he said, made God real and present for his hearers. Fuchs, concentrating mostly on Jesus' *conduct*, emphasized his table-fellowship with publicans and sinners, his seeking out of the last, the least and the lost. Here, he said, we see One who acts in God's place and accomplishes his saving work. This is 'the goodness of God in action'.

Both Bornkamm and Fuchs agreed that the implicit eschatological understanding of Jesus' person and mission, which the disciples gained from Jesus himself, contains 'indirect Christology' which became explicit in the preaching of the first apostles. Even if Jesus did not claim any Messianic titles, and though the nature of our sources do not allow us to write a biography of Jesus, there is enough good historical evidence to show that the Church's *kerygma* is rooted in the works and words of Jesus himself.

All this is a welcome improvement on Bultmann's thorough-going scepticism. It shows a better understanding of faith and history and suggests a truer Christology. In the eyes of most British scholars Bornkamm's *Jesus of Nazareth* is a big advance on Bultmann's *Jesus and the Word*. We cannot, for example, imagine Bultmann saying, as Bornkamm does, that 'the primitive tradition of Jesus is brim full of history'. Again, whereas for Bultmann Jesus is only one 'historical presupposition' for New Testament theology, for Bornkamm the historical Jesus has become in a real sense its foundation.

One notable feature of the new quest has been its stress on 'existential hermeneutics'.

Herméneus is Greek for interpreter, and traditionally 'hermeneutics' has been the science of interpretation. In our time the old word has been re-pristinated by Bultmann and his followers to denote the interpretation of Biblical meanings in modern categories. Chief of these is existentialism. Thus when Bultmann

---

[14] *Jesus of Nazareth.*   [15] *Studies of the Historical Jesus.*

says that 'Jesus' words are not didactic propositions but an invitation and a call to decision', this is an existentialist's way of putting things, but who will say that it is not a true judgment? If to think existentially is to think not as a spectator of the ultimate issues of life and death but as one committed to a decision on them; and if it is existentialist teaching that knowledge of God and his truth becomes ours only in the act of deciding for it with 'all that in us is', then, by the witness of the Gospels, Jesus was an existentialist.

The new hermeneutics owe much also to the new idea of history enunciated by men like Dilthey and Collingwood. In the nineteenth century the so-called 'scientific historians' regarded their business as primarily the quest for the 'brute facts' and the cause-effect series of events. According to the new view, the historian's business is to re-enact the past in his own mind by re-thinking it, and to discover and experience it personally. His concern should be not so much for the 'outside' as for the 'inside' of events, since the essence of history lies in the purpose and meanings of selves. In their actions persons reveal themselves, so that the historian's aim should be to re-create the existential understandings of past human beings.

In view of all this, the task of the New Testament exegete is to 'interpret the phenomena of past history (i.e. Jesus and his story) in the light of man's understanding of his existence' and so, 'by making the past live again, bring home to us the truth, *Tua res agitur*, it concerns yourself'.[16]

Such are the new hermeneutics which Bultmann's successors are now applying to the Gospels; and in the pages of a scholar like Bornkamm they take on a new attractiveness because he has seen, as Bultmann did not, that the kingdom of God in Jesus' teaching is a dawning reality, and not merely a future hope.

What does it mean to read the Gospels thus? Just as long ago Jesus confronted men in his deeds and words with the reality, presence and grace of God, so that he challenged them to the response of faith, so still today Jesus confronts men and calls them to commitment. This encounter with Jesus compels men

---

[16] Bultmann, *Primitive Christianity*, 8.

today, as it did Nicodemus and others long ago, to step out of their customary background, and face up to his challenge and call. Moreover, the Gospels preserve many 'disclosure' sayings and situations in which Jesus' self and intention are made clear. These shed light on Jesus' mind and meaning for today, and so renew the urgency of the old question, 'What think ye of Christ?', and challenge us to decision in the living present.

This new way of reading the Gospels has obvious merits. It does not do away with the old historical criticism; but that criticism, ceasing to be an end in itself, becomes a means of letting the Gospels confront us with Jesus as the One who brings God near and makes him real in the present. So it brings us face to face with the *Mysterium Christi*. What manner of man is this who can so act, so speak, as thus to make God real and relevant, for blessing or for judgment?

Such are the new hermeneutics as practised by 'the new questers'. How shall we judge of them? First, they represent an advance on the methods of the 'old questers'. The Liberal scholars tended to separate Jesus' words from the mystery of his being, and so, by effacing his character as the Christ, to turn him into a teacher of ethical truths. But, as 'the new questers' realize, *being* comes before speaking, and often the secret of Jesus' being is enclosed in his words. Again, the Liberals tended to detach Jesus' actions from his being, and to see his conduct simply as an ethical example to be imitated. But, as Fuchs and Bornkamm emphasize, Jesus' actions, as interpreted by his sayings and parables, are the expression of the mystery of his being. Second, existential hermeneutics, as we have already shown, do make the Jesus of the Gospels 'come alive' with a new relevancy and challenge, even if ultimately this must be the work of God's Holy Spirit. (Stephen Neill[17] characterizes Bultmann's work as 'a gallant attempt . . . to make the challenge existential . . . without a doctrine of the Holy Spirit'.)

In the foregoing paragraphs we have sought to do justice to the work of the men engaged on the 'new quest'. Nevertheless, for all its merits, this Bultmannian 'revisionism', as we prefer to call it,

[17] *The Interpretation of the New Testament*, 1861-1961, 233.

even as practised by so sincere and humble a Christian as Born-kamm, cannot be called satisfactory.

For one thing, it is still vitiated by Bultmann's 'disseminated scepticism'. Even Bornkamm, who has recanted a good deal of it, must be faulted here. A good example is his view of the title Son of Man. 'I consider', he writes,[18] 'it probable that the historical Jesus never used the title "Son of Man" of himself.' For Born-kamm the title is the creation of the primitive Church. This indurated scepticism quite fails to reckon with the remarkable fact that in all our Gospels the title is used by Jesus of himself many times, but is never once used by anyone else as a form of address to him. On the other hand, except for a solitary use of it by the proto-martyr Stephen in Acts 7.56, the title was apparently never applied to Jesus by the early Christians. In fine, Bornkamm's view is a piece of special pleading which has all the probabilities against it.

But perhaps the biggest problem the new questers have on their hands is that of 'the two avenues of encounter with Jesus'.[19] On the one hand, they tell us that the Christian knows Christ through the *kerygma*, existentially. On the other hand, they tell us that faith and theology have their saving centre in a historical person who is accessible to 'scientific historiography'. This difficulty they resolve by allowing 'scientific history' to shape the knowledge of Jesus we have through the *kerygma*. And all this though we are told that faith does not depend on such historiography!

On examination it turns out that what they mean by 'scientific history' is really the old nineteenth-century positivistic view of history which found no place for the activity of God in it and dogmatically declared that miracles were impossible. The difficulty of their whole position comes to a head when they discuss the Resurrection of Jesus. Their 'scientific history' will not allow them to speak of it as a historical event. Yet, as Alan Richardson[20] rightly says, there is no *scientific* presupposition of the historical method which requires the historian to rule out the possibility of divine action in history, such as God's raising of Jesus from the

---

[18] *Jesus of Nazareth*, 230.   [19] Robinson, *The New Quest*, 85f.
[20] *History Sacred and Profane*, 152f.

dead. In other words, it is not historical method but their own positivistic view of history which makes the 'new questers' say the Resurrection is not a historical event. To accept such a view is to fall prey to dispiriting fables about the world as a closed continuum of cause and effect in which the arm of the Lord is powerless to save. It is in fact to give up the Christian view of God as the Lord of history.

IV

A quest to be resumed

But, in spite of 'the new hermeneutic', is all this talk of a new quest really justified ? Most British scholars and continentals like Jeremias and Cullmann have never been with the prodigal son (Bultmann) in the 'far country' of historical scepticism, and do not need, like the grandsons (Käsemann, etc.), to wend a slow and weary way back. The findings of the early Form Critics may have temporarily shaken us in our quest; but after forty years we may fairly claim to have taken the measure of their weaknesses as well as their strengths. Form Criticism need not lead to historical scepticism; properly applied, it may be a useful tool in the critic's hand. Ought we not therefore now to be resuming the old quest, taking good care this time to avoid the errors of our predecessors, and especially that of modernizing Jesus ?

Moreover, there are sound reasons for re-embarking on the quest with good hope. Though we may criticize the Liberal scholars who pioneered the original quest, we may be grateful to them nevertheless. To them we owe in large measure what we may call the assured results of source criticism – the priority of Mark and the probability of 'Q'. To these we may add the insights into the formation of the oral tradition which the Form Critics have given us. Thanks to Otto, Dodd, Kümmel and others we may now claim to understand the eschatology of the Gospels much better. Background research into Jewish apocalyptic and rabbinical theology, together with the new light thrown on contemporary sectarian Judaism by the Dead Sea Scrolls, now enable us to see the ministry of Jesus in a truer setting. The Aramaic approach to

the Gospels by Dalman, Jeremias and Black has thrown welcome
light on the sayings of Jesus at this point and that. Finally, in the
last decade or two a 'new look' has been coming over the Fourth
Gospel. No longer can we curtly dismiss it, as Kirsopp Lake did
in the 'forties', as 'mostly fiction'. Recent work by Dodd and
Raymond Brown has led to a fresh evaluation of the historical
worth of the Gospel.[21] With these new helps and safeguards, with
these sharpened techniques and new materials, we may now go
forward in the confidence that 'the dawn which arose in Palestine
has still to unfold its greater splendours', and that historical
criticism has its own part to play in dissipating the shadows.

We hold, therefore, that it is necessary to know what the Jesus
of history said and did if our *kerygma* is to have a firm foundation.
We do not hold that historical research can of itself prove that God
acted in the history of Jesus and that this history is the final
revelation of God. For this the leap of Christian faith is necessary,
but it is not a leap in the dark. The assertion, so often made nowadays, that faith is completely independent of historical criticism,
is simply not true.

What then can historical criticism tell us about the Jesus of
history? Suppose, for argument's sake, that we accept the general
view of 'the new questers' that Jesus never claimed the Messianic
titles of majesty found on his lips in the Gospels – that the early
Church in fact put them there. Even so, it is possible to uncover in
Jesus' words and deeds much 'indirect christology'.

All the new questers agree that Jesus confronted men in his
words and deeds with a quite astounding authority. Here is how
three of them express themselves:

'Jesus', says Fuchs,[22] 'appears as One who acts in God's place,
summoning to him sinners who without him would have to flee
from God.'

'In Jesus himself', says Bornkamm,[23] 'the dawn of the Kingdom
of God becomes a reality. To make the reality of God present:
this is the essential mystery of Jesus.' And this he does by 'opening
up to men a new relationship with God' and giving them 'the

---

[21] See my book *According to John*. [22] *Studies of the Historical Jesus*, 21.
[23] *Jesus of Nazareth*, 62, 170.

possibility of a new being in the present'. Käsemann,[24] commenting on Jesus' 'But I say unto you', declares: 'He who does what is done here has cut himself off from the community of Judaism – or else he brings the Messianic Torah and is therefore the Messiah . . . The only category which does justice to his claim (quite independently of whether he used it himself or required it of others) is that in which his disciples themselves placed him – namely, that of the Messiah.'

Put these judgments together – One who acts in God's stead, appearing as the incarnate goodness of God: One who makes the reality of God present in his own person and opens up a new relationship for man with God: One for whom the only right theological category is that of Messiah – and they surely attest a claim by the Jesus of history to a place in the Good News he proclaimed, not unworthy of the central position he was to hold, after the Resurrection, in the proclamation of the apostles.

But we can go further. The Jesus of the Gospels and the message he preached have no parallel in Judaism. Search Jewish literature, and you will find no parallel to the message that Jesus brings – that God in his sheer grace is now offering his salvation to the last, the least and the lost, and promising them a share in the Kingdom of God which is now dawning. Search Jewish literature, and you will not find anywhere in it what you find in the parables of Luke 15 – not the preaching of the timeless idea of a loving Father in heaven, but the declaration that the heavenly Father's love is now becoming a glad reality in the mission and message of the Speaker. Search Jewish literature, and you will look in vain for a man who prefaces his words with an 'Amen I say unto you',[25] who dares to address God as Abba,[26] who tells his disciples that he alone knows the Almighty as Father and for this knowledge all men must become debtors to him (Matt. 11.27. Q).[27]

[24] *Essays on New Testament Themes*, 37f.

[25] The Jews used Amen, as we do, at the end of a prayer or scripture reading. It was the sign of the congregation's assent. Jesus – and there is no parallel in Judaism to his usage – sets the word at the beginning of his saying. By so doing he shows that his proclamation is not his own but God's, that he only passes on what he receives. ('Here,' says Schlier, 'is Christology *in nuce*.')

[26] On this see Jeremias, *The Prayers of Jesus*, 11–65.

[27] On the authenticity of Matt. 11.25ff. see my *Teaching and Preaching the New Testament*, 41–50.

So we might multiply the evidence, but the result is ever the same. As we study the historical Jesus with the aid of critical scholarship, we find ourselves in the presence of God himself. Behind the words and deeds of Jesus in the Gospels lies the claim to be the uniquely accredited Representative of 'the Lord of heaven and earth' who is now bringing his kingdom and salvation to men. This unique claim is the very basis and foundation of Christianity; and therefore the study of the Jesus of history is no mere marginal task for New Testament scholarship, but its chief concern.

We come back then to the palmary question of the continuity between the historical Jesus and the *kerygma* of the apostles. In *The Riddle of the New Testament*,[28] Hoskyns and Davey put the problem clearly:

Any historical reconstruction which leaves an unbridgeable gap between the faith of the primitive church (i.e. the *kerygma*) and the historical Jesus must be both inadequate and uncritical: inadequate because it leaves the origin of the Church unexplained, and uncritical because a critical sifting of the New Testament points towards the life and death of Jesus as the ground of primitive Christian faith, and points in no other direction.

This is unquestionably true. On this score Bultmann's 'historical reconstruction' falls down so badly that his pupils have made it a prime point of their studies to show that there must be a correspondence between the Jesus of history and the apostles' preaching of him; that, to put it otherwise, Jesus of Nazareth must somehow have been big enough to bear the weight of the terrific claims made for him by the apostles.

But if what we have said about the historical Jesus be true, if he made the unique claim which we have suggested, he is not unworthy. And this is profoundly important, because, whereas Jesus' 'good news' without the *kerygma* of the apostles is dead, the apostles' *kerygma* without Jesus' 'good news' is only the proclamation of an idea.

The Gospel of Jesus and the *kerygma* of the apostles then belong together, and may not be isolated. On the other hand, they

[28] p. 246f.

are not on the same footing. As Jeremias[29] puts it, they stand to each other as Call and Response:

The life, acts and death of Jesus, the authoritative word of him who dared to say Abba, the one who with Divine authority invited sinners to his table, and as the Servant of God went to the Cross, is the Call of God. The early Church's proclamation of faith, the Spirit-led chorus of a thousand tongues, is the Answer to God's Call . . .

Jesus of Nazareth is God's Call, confession of him is the Response. This Response has a double aspect: it is praise and adoration of God, and witness to the world. It is inspired by the Spirit of God, but it does not take the place of the Call. The Call, not the Response, is the decisive thing. The many-sided confession of faith of the early Church, of Paul, of John, of the Epistle to the Hebrews, must be judged in the light of the message of Jesus.

In fine, the historical Jesus and his message is not one pre-supposition among many for the *Kerygma*, but its sole presupposition.

V

Practical conclusions

Now, by way of epilogue, let us ask what practical conclusions follow from this discussion of the quest for the historical Jesus.

The first one seems to me to be this. *If the ordinary Christian is not to worship a semi-mythological Lord, he must have some knowledge of the Jesus of history.*

Right from the beginning the Church realized this. The Gospels themselves are evidence that the earliest preachers did not deem it sufficient to preach Christ as 'a faceless eschatological event'. Rather they show how necessary it was that converts should know how the Lord whom they confessed had come to the Cross, how he had lived, what he had taught. It did matter that they should understand how the Lord Jesus, in the days of his flesh, had dealt with all sorts and conditions of men – with fisherfolk called to be disciples, cripples and sorrowing parents, grasping publicans and religious bigots, penitents and little children. And it mattered because this same Jesus was the risen

[29] 'The Present Position in the Controversy Concerning the Problem of the Historical Jesus' in the *Expository Times*, August 1958, p. 339.

One who had given an example to be followed by the Church of which he was now the exalted Head.[30]

Is this not still true today? Does not 'the moral appeal of the Jesus of history' still remain a potent factor in leading men to confess him as their Saviour and Lord, just because he is the Jesus of history, and not the semi-mythical hero of some Palestinian morality play?

By all means let us be grateful for the rediscovery in our day of the apostolic Gospel, the *kerygma*. This has led to much preaching of 'the mighty acts of God' – the Incarnation, the Cross, the Resurrection, the Exaltation. But such preaching, if it ignores or despises the historical Jesus, can be dangerously one-sided. Some knowledge of the earthly ministry of the Church's Lord is needed, precisely because (in John Baillie's words[31]) 'not just that a Saviour came, but the kind of Saviour he was – not just that God was incarnate in a man but the kind of man in which he was incarnate, constitutes the essence of the good news'. It was the Jesus of history, and none other, who died and rose again. It would not have been the Christian revelation as we know it if, say, it had been one of the two thieves – even the penitent one – who had died for us and been raised again. So writes Dr Lillie,[32] and he goes on to add: 'Some of us, as we look back, can equally see how faith in Jesus and a love to him had their beginnings in our own hearts as we heard in childhood the stories of his earthly ministry, even although at that time we naturally had little understanding of what the Cross meant to him or to us.'

The second conclusion is a corollary of the first. *The modern preacher must not only proclaim 'the mighty acts of God' in Christ, he must also 'preach Jesus' – portray the life and person of Jesus as we know him from the Gospels.*

For this we have New Testament warrant – it was the apostolic way. According to Luke (see Acts 10.36-39), St Peter did it. St John did it, teaching theology by biography – if we may believe, as I think we may, that he is the 'authority' behind the Fourth Gospel. The Writer to the Hebrews was not afraid to appeal to

---

[30] Alan Richardson, *History Sacred and Profane*, 240.
[31] *The Sense of the Presence of God*, 210.   [32] *Jesus Then and Now*, 10.

'the days of his flesh' and 'the obedience Jesus learned in the school of suffering'. And even Paul, who is sometimes cited as the preacher *par excellence* of 'the mighty acts of God' shows in his letters that he was far from ignorant of our Lord's character and teaching.

Why must we 'preach Jesus' – the historical Jesus in the days of his flesh? For the simple but sufficient reason that if we confine ourselves to 'the mighty acts of God', we shall tend to replace faith in a personal God and a personal Saviour with some kind of mechanical doctrine of salvation. To be sure, the preaching of the historical Jesus can be fraught with dangers. Many who have done so have sentimentalized him, romanticized him, psychologized him. But if we remain silent about the historical Jesus – say nothing in our sermons about 'the strong Son of God' who

> wrought
> With human hands the creed of creeds
> In loveliness of perfect deeds

we shall be in danger of proclaiming what Dr Lillie calls 'a dehydrated Gospel' in which Jesus becomes an unknown 'x' playing a mysterious part in a depersonalized scheme of salvation.

By all means let us learn from the practitioners of the 'new hermeneutics' how to make this preaching of the historical Jesus existential and challenging – a sword to pierce our hearers' hearts, a Word of God which, uttered long ago in Galilee, becomes a call in the living present to bewildered twentieth-century man. But let us remember that, though the word be modern, the existential note has always characterized Christian preaching at its best. When Richard Baxter

> preach'd as never sure to preach again
> And as a dying man to dying men

he was most certainly preaching existentially. And the same may be said today of any preaching of the Man Jesus which makes the old, old stories come alive, speak to our present condition, and confront men with the grace and judgment of God in Jesus his incarnate, crucified and risen Son.

A word of epilogue on Bultmann's demythologizing proposals.

To 'demyth' or not to 'demyth', that is the question Bultmann puts to the preacher. How shall we answer it?

There is demythologizing and demythologizing. There is the kind that every preacher worthy of his salt does almost unconsciously, and has been doing for a long time before Bultmann wrote his celebrated essay. Every preacher, save the most incurable literalist, does it when he talks, for example, about the Ascension. But this is quite another matter from assenting to Bultmann's invitation to reinterpret the mythological formulation of the New Testament Gospel in *abstract* Heideggerian terms. (This reflects the intellectual movement of our time – abstract art, atonal music, scientific formulae, mathematical thinking. All reveal a great undertow of abstraction. This has led to a loss of concrete history and vivid reality. We have lost our 'names' and been given numbers instead. In place of what we can grasp with our senses – melody, imagery, space and time, we have been given figures, notions, formulae, etc. Bultmann's existential interpretation shares in this intellectual background which threatens to dissolve history into the mere historicity of human existence.[33])

To endorse Bultmann's proposals in their entirety is, in fact, to run the risk of preaching 'another Gospel' – a Gospel of self-salvation in which Jesus becomes simply the opportunity for man to save himself by making the right decision. On the contrary, we must insist that the Christian religion, when it faces the problem of expressing the transcendent and ineffable, must resort to 'myth' – that is, the expression in story form of theological truth that cannot readily be communicated in any other way.

Dr R. W. Stewart, recalling Gerard Manley Hopkins' invocation of the Deity as 'Sir' and some modern churchmen's preference for 'You' to 'Thou' in addressing God, sums up much of the modern discussion in some verses which are both witty and true:

'Tell me thy name', so wrestling Jacob prayed.
Sir, have a heart. Tell me the magic word
That means that when it's uttered all is said,
A deep reverberating final chord.
Father? Too human! Demythologize it!

[33] See Zahrnt, *The Historical Jesus*, 91f.

But did not Jesus, dying, authorize it?
After the swirling doubt and dark despair
And mortal cry, his quiet, final prayer
Was, 'Father into thy hands I
Commend my spirit ere I die.'
Hands? Do we then mean fingers, thumbs?
Anthropomorphic it becomes.
Why not? If Jesus be divine,
Through flesh men saw God's glory shine.
Macluhan! Is your slogan really new?
Christ is God's medium and his message too.
The curly-scented petals don't enclose
A flower within: the petals *are* the rose.
Myth is the language that contains the clue
To that which is at once both real and true.
If Jesus' word is, 'In my Father's house
Are many mansions' is it any use
In prose or purely abstract phraseology
To seek a better bottom for theology?

BIBLIOGRAPHY

ALBRIGHT, W. F., *Archaeology of Palestine*, Penguin Books, 1949
ANDERSON, H., *Jesus and Christian Origins*, OUP, 1964

BAILLIE, JOHN, *The Sense of the Presence of God*, OUP, 1962
BARCLAY, WILLIAM, *Daily Study Bible Series*, St Andrew Press and
  Westminster Press, Philadelphia, 1953 ff.
BARRY, F. R., *The Relevance of Christianity*, James Nisbet, 1931. US
  title,
  Christianity and the New World, Harper & Bros, 1932
BERNARD, J. H., *St John*, T. & T. Clark and Charles Scribner's Sons,
  NY, 1928
Bible Day by Day, The, Church of Scotland Publications
BLACK, M., *An Aramaic Approach to the Gospels and Acts*[3], OUP, 1967
BORNKAMM, GÜNTHER, *Jesus of Nazareth*, Hodder & Stoughton and
  Harper & Row, NY, 1960
BULTMANN, RUDOLF, *Jesus and the Word*, Nicholson & Watson and
  Charles Scribner's Sons, 1935
  Kerygma and History (ed. Braaten & Harrisville), Abingdon Press,
  NY 1962
  Kerygma and Myth, SPCK and Harper & Row, 1953
  Primitive Christianity, Collins and Meridian Books, NY, 1960
  Theology of the New Testament, SCM Press and Charles Scribner's
  Sons. Vol I, 1952, Vol II, 1955
BURNEY, C. F., *The Poetry of Our Lord*, OUP, 1925

CAIRD, G. B., *St Luke*, Penguin Books, 1963
CAIRNS, DAVID, *A Gospel Without Myth?*, SCM Press, 1960
CAMPENHAUSEN, H. VON, *Tradition and Life in the Church*, Collins and
  Fortress Press, Philadelphia, 1968

DENNEY, JAMES, *The Way Everlasting*, Hodder & Stoughton, 1911
DODD, C. H., *Historical Tradition in the Fourth Gospel*, CUP, 1963
  Studies in the Gospels, Basil Blackwell, 1955

FORSYTH, P. T., *Positive Preaching and the Modern Mind*, Hodder & Stoughton, 1907
FUCHS, ERNST, *Studies of the Historical Jesus*, SCM Press, 1964

GLOVER, T. R., *The Jesus of History*, SCM Press, 1917

HEIDEGGER, MARTIN, *Being and Time*, SCM Press and Harper & Row, 1962 and Basil Blackwell, 1963
HOSKYNS, E., and DAVY, F. N., *The Riddle of the New Testament*, Faber & Faber, 3rd ed. 1947
HUNTER, A. M., *According to John*, SCM Press and Westminster Press, 1968
   Design for Life, SCM Press, 1953. US title, *A Pattern for Life*, Westminster Press
   Teaching and Preaching the New Testament, SCM Press and Westminster Press, 1963
   The Work and Words of Jesus, SCM Press and Westminster Press, 1950

JEREMIAS, JOACHIM, *The Eucharistic Words of Jesus*, SCM Press and Charles Scribner's Sons, Rev. ed. 1966
   The Prayers of Jesus, SCM Press, 1967
   Rediscovering the Parables, SCM Press and Charles Scribner's Sons, 1966

KÄSEMANN, ERNST, *Essays on New Testament Themes*, SCM Press, 1964
KLAUSNER, J., *Jesus of Nazareth*, Allen & Unwin and The Macmillan Co., NY, 1929

Layman's Bible Commentaries, SCM Press and John Knox Press, Richmond, Virginia, 1960-65
LEWIS, C. S., *Miracles*, Geoffrey Bles and The Macmillan Co., 1957
LILLIE, W., *Jesus Then and Now*, SPCK and Westminster Press, 1964

MACQUARRIE, JOHN, *Martin Heidegger*, Lutterworth Press and John Knox Press, 1968
MANSON, T. W., *The Background and Eschatology of the New Testament*, CUP, 1956
   Ethics and the Gospel, SCM Press and Charles Scribner's Sons, 1960
   The Sayings of Jesus, SCM Press and E. P. Dutton & Co., NY, 1949
   The Teaching of Jesus, CUP, 2nd ed. 1935
MOULE, C. F. D., *The Birth of the New Testament*, A. & C. Black, 2nd ed. 1966, and Harper & Row
MUGGERIDGE, MALCOLM, *Another King*, St Andrew Press, 1968
MURRY, MIDDLETON, *The Life of Jesus*, Jonathan Cape, 1926

Bibliography

NEIL, WILLIAM, *The New Testament in Historical and Contemporary Perspective*, Basil Blackwell, 1965

NEILL, STEPHEN, *The Interpretation of the New Testament*, OUP, 1964

PEDDIE, CAMERON, *The Forgotten Talent*, Oldbourne Press, 1961

RICHARDSON, ALAN, *History Sacred and Profane*, SCM Press and Westminster Press, 1964
The Miracles Stories of the Gospels, SCM Press, 1941

ROBINSON, JAMES M., *A New Quest of the Historical Jesus*, SCM Press, 1959

SCHWEITZER, ALBERT, *The Quest of the Historical Jesus*, A. & C. Black and The Macmillan Co., 1911

SMITH, C. W. F., *The Jesus of the Parables*, Westminster Press, 1958

TAYLOR, THOMAS M., *Where One Man Stands*, St Andrew Press, 1960

TEMPLE, WILLIAM, *Readings in St John's Gospel*, Macmillan & Co. and St Martin's Press, NY, 1942

Theologische Wörterbuch zum Neuen Testament (TWNT), ed. G. Kittel, Kohlhammer, Stuttgart, 1932 ff.

Torch Bible Commentaries, SCM Press, 1948 ff.

Vindications, ed. Anthony Hanson, SCM Press and Morehouse-Barlow, NY, 1966

ZAHRNT, H., *The Historical Jesus*, Collins and Harper & Row, 1963

INDEX OF SUBJECTS

INDEX OF AUTHORS

Index of Authors

Newman, 21
Nineham, 40

Paley, 87
Papias, 34
Peddie, 92
Queen Mother, 107

Reimarus, 119
Renan, 120
Richardson, 87, 130, 136
Riesenfeld, 39
Robinson, J. M., 39, 119, 126

Schmidt, 37
Schweitzer, 48, 57, 120ff.
Scott, Sir Walter, 2

Seeley, Sir J. R., 120
Smith, C. W. F., 106
Smith, W. R., 3
Stewart, R. W., 138f.
Strauss, 120

Taylor, Sir T. M., 113
Temple, W., 121
Tertullian, 101
Thielicke, 68

Von Campenhausen, 109f., 111

Wesley, John, 72
Wodehouse, 96

Zahrnt, 138

5535-14
119